LAW OF THE LAND

A Practical Legal Guide for Tourists and Business Travelers

Greece

By Michael L. Moore Esq.

DEDICATION

This book is dedicated to the memory of my late older brother, Kenneth Lee Moore, whose tragic murder at 15 years of age inspired me to write this series of books.

This book is also dedicated to my parents, John Henry Moore, and Edna Mae Moore, whose tremendous parenting skills kept me focused on the important things in life: being reverent, getting educated, and prioritizing family.

Finally, this book is dedicated to my beautiful family, my wife Royellen, my son AJ, and my daughter Karla. They inspire me every single day to be kind, patient, and compassionate.

IN LOVING MEMORY OF:

Belinda Joyce Moore Moss—my beautiful and wonderful sister, who supported me in every positive thing that I ever attempted to do.

Michael Eugene Baker—my dedicated and loyal friend and brother, who always wanted the very best for me.

Sylvia Joyce Hill—my eldest sister, who had a beautiful spirit and was like a second mother to me.

LAW OF THE LAND®

PUBLISHING for Tourists & Business Travelers

Travel smart. Stay legal. Stay safe.®

From local laws to medical guides
we've got you covered world wide
in one digital platform.

PREFACE

My introduction to the justice system came when I was only 10 years old. My 15-year-old brother was murdered with a butcher knife by a 19-year-old in a simple argument over a torn shirt. I was devastated by his death and sought retribution for his fate that never came. The woman was initially charged with second degree murder, but after plea negotiations, she was convicted of manslaughter and sentenced to only five years in a youthful offender school and ordered to undergo psychiatric care. That was it. Nothing more. The judicial system had run its course.

My family knew nothing about the justice system, and we did not have the tools to advocate for ourselves. No one provided us with a written source to reference for guidance through this process. There was no easily accessible, easy to understand, definitive source to educate ourselves about the legal system that we suddenly and unexpectedly found ourselves immersed in after being victimized by such a violent criminal act.

As I got older, finished college, law school, and ultimately started practicing law, it became clear to me that most people are not knowledgeable about the law or how the judicial process works. If most people are uninformed here in the United States regarding the law and the legal process, how would they fare when in other countries? I realized that tourists and businesspeople who travel internationally needed access to information on how to navigate the legal system in other countries!

For many years, there has been considerable media attention focused on international travelers experiencing legal difficulties while traveling abroad. Most of these news stories gained attention in the United States and abroad because they involved American citizens facing punishment that was considered "unconventional" and "harsh" by United States' legal standards. I recall a news story in 1994 regarding Michael Fay, a young American male, who had broken the law in Singapore. He was convicted and sentenced to be caned and or whipped publicly. While the United States Government weighed in on the inappropriate and cruel nature of the punishment, the young American was beaten because he had been convicted under Singapore law.

Similarly, in recent years, international news stories have garnered headlines regarding foreign travelers and their issues with the laws of countries that were not their own. Amanda Knox, an American woman, was accused of murdering her roommate in Italy in 2007 and spent almost four years in an Italian prison before being definitively acquitted by the Supreme Court of Cassatio. Kenneth Bae, an American citizen, was arrested in North Korea in 2012 and was convicted for hostile acts against the communist country. He was sentenced to 15 years hard labor but was released in 2014 after efforts by the U.S. State Department. More recently, United States Basketball Star, Brittany Griner was arrested in February 2022 at a Moscow airport on drug-related charges and detained for nearly 10 months, spending much of that time in prison. Her plight unfolded at the same time Russia invaded Ukraine and further heightened tensions between Russia and the United States, ending only after she was freed in exchange for a notorious Russian arms dealer.

It was in 1994 that another personal tragic event occurred that finally inspired me to write these series of books. A dear friend and also client of mine was brutally murdered while on his second honeymoon in Jamaica. News of his murder shocked me and our local community. The legal hurdles his family had to overcome to see that justice was properly dispensed far away from home, in another country, with an entirely different set of criminal procedural rules and laws, was difficult to navigate.

As I was my friend's attorney at the time of his death, his family asked that I act as their "legal liaison" to the Jamaican Prosecutor's Office and to the Jamaican Police Department. I participated in multiple police interviews with my client's widow because she was the primary witness to his murder. As a former prosecuting attorney, I was also allowed by the Court, as a professional courtesy, to sit at the prosecutor's table to consult with the prosecuting attorney during trial. What I observed about the Jamaican trial process from a front row seat was compelling enough to cause me to seriously consider educating the "world" regarding what to expect and how to act appropriately when faced with legal issues while traveling abroad.

One of the realities in life is that, regardless of what country you are in, it is never a pleasant experience to run afoul of the law and be forced to accept that someone else will be making a decision about your pecuniary, proprietary, or penal interests (your money, your property, or your freedom).

It is important to know what the laws are, how they apply to you, and how to navigate the legal system if you are charged with a crime. It is also very helpful to know what resources are available to you if you are the victim of a criminal act. At the end of the day, an "ounce of prevention is worth a pound of cure," so the more knowledge you have, the more ammunition you possess, and the more likely you will have a positive outcome.

If you are traveling to Greece, the first thing you should pack is a copy of this book! The helpful information and tips contained in this volume will provide a great starting point for knowing what to do (and not to do!) when you arrive at your destination and will help ensure that you have a wonderful vacation or business trip unmarred by tangles with the law.

TABLE OF CONTENTS

INTRODUCTION

INTRODUCTION

As a practicing attorney for over 34 years, I have encountered numerous clients who travel often, but are unaware of the laws of the land they are traveling to.

Therefore, many years ago, I decided to write a series of books that would explain the laws of specific countries. My focus was to explain the laws that may affect travelers in a straightforward manner, without all of the legal language that is sometimes hard for even seasoned attorneys to understand.

About This Book

The aim of this book is simple. It provides you, the traveler, with a simple, easy to read book that will provide a basic legal guide that explains the law in the country that you are about to visit. It is not intended to educate you on ALL of the laws in a given country. The goal is to provide you with the details of the most common legal and safety issues faced by tourists and business travelers.

I have also provided context with background information on places not to visit, statistics on the country and prevention measures you should take to safeguard your legal and physical safety. Knowledge is a powerful thing and knowing how to stay out of trouble (or how to get out of it!) is important for everyone who travels.

This *Law of The Land/Greece* book simply helps you become more informed about your legal rights, responsibilities, and obligations in a wide range of subject areas.

Last, but not least, this book does NOT purport to offer legal advice. It does, however, provide the information you need to stay safe, follow the law and navigate around legal difficulties. However, if you do face legal difficulties, the information in this book will provide you with a starting point for solving the problem and obtaining legal assistance should it be required.

Hypotheticals Used Throughout This Book

From time to time throughout this book, I will explain the law to readers by using hypothetical scenarios. These hypotheticals will be marked by an icon that will be explained in further detail as you read on.

How This Book is Organized

CHAPTER 1: **About Greece.** This chapter will provide you with a brief overview about Greece and its history. It also addresses Visa requirements, monetary advice, and the best times to visit.

CHAPTER 2: **Customs.** This chapter will provide information on what to expect when entering Greece. It will also explain what restricted and prohibited items are when entering Greece along with customs regulations.

CHAPTER 3: **Crime in Greece.** This chapter provides an overview of the history of crime in Greece and steps that Greek officials have taken to curb the high rate of crime.

CHAPTER 4: **Criminal Law Violations.** This chapter will provide information on drug offenses, penalties, true events, and questions and answers.

CHAPTER 5: **Alcohol-Related Offenses.** This chapter will provide key points regarding the sale, consumption, and regulations of alcohol use in Greece.

CHAPTER 6: **Firearm & Ammunition Offenses.** This chapter will provide key points regarding the possession of firearms and ammunition in Greece.

CHAPTER 7: **Prostitution.** This chapter provides an overview of the history of prostitution in Greece, laws and penalties, prostitution practices, sex trafficking, sex tourism, health in Greece, tips to avoid being hassled, a Law of the Land Hypothetical, and the current situation on prostitution in Greece.

CHAPTER 8: **LGBTQ.** This chapter will provide information regarding the acceptance of LGBTQ people in Greece, and the laws surrounding homosexuality.

CHAPTER 9: **Sexually Motivated/Violent Crimes.** This chapter will provide an overview of sexually related crimes in Greece.

CHAPTER 10: **Arrested in Greece.** This chapter will provide information on what to do if you are arrested in Greece.

CHAPTER 11: **Jails vs. Prisons: Conditions & Culture.** This chapter will provide information on the conditions and culture of Greek Jails and Prisons.

CHAPTER 12: **Helping a Friend or Relative Imprisoned in Greece.** This chapter will provide information on how you can assist a friend or relative imprisoned in Greece.

CHAPTER 13: **The Administration of Justice.** This chapter will provide information on Greece's Judicial System.

CHAPTER 14: **Crime Victim Assistance.** This chapter will provide information on crime victim assistance along with providing safety tips.

LAW OF THE LAND GREECE

CHAPTER 15: **Police.** This chapter will provide information on the Greek Police and how to report a crime.

CHAPTER 16: **How to Get Legal Help in Greece.** This chapter will provide information regarding how to obtain legal assistance for travelers to Greece.

CHAPTER 17: **Medical Facilities & Hospitals.** This chapter will provide information about how to obtain medical care while visiting Greece.

CHAPTER 18: **Driving in Greece.** This chapter will provide information on driving in Greece, traffic rules, and road safety tips.

CHAPTER 19: **Nude Beaches & Clothing-Optional Resorts.** This chapter will provide an overview of nude beaches and clothing-optional resorts in Greece, and the legality and safety of visiting nude beaches in Greece.

CHAPTER 20: **Unusual Laws.** This chapter will provide information on some Unusual Laws in Greece, and penalties and fines.

CHAPTER 21: **Traveling Safely.** This chapter will provide information on women traveling alone, crime prevention for families, safety notes for all travelers, and overall advice.

CHAPTER 22: **Tourist Taxation.** This chapter will provide information on taxes that tourists are required to pay in Greece.

CHAPTER 23: **Long-Term Stays.** This chapter will provide an overview of the consequences for overstaying your visit to Greece.

CHAPTER 24: **Civil Litigation.** This chapter will provide information about the civil litigation process in Greece.

CHAPTER 25: **Other Things to Know.** This chapter will provide information on the harassment of tourists, travel and safety, and other practical tips.

CHAPTER 26: **Quick Reference Guide.** This chapter is a quick way to get information. It is a condensed version of the chapters in this book.

Emergency/Important Contact Numbers in Greece

Useful Greek Phrases

Glossary

Icons Used in this Book

What do those pictures throughout the book mean? See below:

WARNING: This icon flags information about things you should **avoid** while visiting Greece. Heed the advice next to this icon to avoid legal perils.

REMEMBER: This icon flags noteworthy information that you **shouldn't forget**.

HELPFUL TIPS: This icon flags information that will help you when entering Greece, relates to a legal situation, or refers to resources available while visiting Greece.

TECHNICAL INFORMATION: This icon flags technical aspects of the law. If you are faced with a legal problem, and you want to learn more about the law involved, this information can be helpful.

 **ADDITIONAL INFORMATION**: This icon points to the location of additional information available on the internet.

 **HYPOTHETICAL**: This icon points to hypothetical scenarios to illustrate possible legal problems and the outcome.

 **QUESTIONS**: This icon points to questions and answers throughout the book.

 **TRUE STORY**: This icon points to true events throughout the book.

Where to Go From Here

If you have a specific question about the law in Greece as it relates to a specific area, just turn to the chapter that addresses that issue, or turn to the Quick Reference Guide. You can also read the book from cover to cover to obtain a more comprehensive understanding of the Greek laws and resources available should you find yourself in a legal predicament while visiting.

 **Disclaimer:** While the recommendations in this book primarily address U.S. citizens, the information is relevant and applicable to citizens of any country.

ABOUT GREECE

ABOUT GREECE

About Greece

Located in Southeastern Europe along the Balkan Peninsula and surrounded by the stunning Ionian and Mediterranean seas, Greece is a top destination for travelers worldwide. This peninsular nation features an archipelago of approximately 3,000 islands, offering an expansive 131,957 km² (50,949 sq. mi) of diverse terrain to explore. With a population of 10,276,2101[1] (2024 estimate), Greece boasts vibrant streets teeming with culture and activity.

Renowned for its rich culture, storied history, and exquisite spirits, Greece offers visitors an array of experiences—from savoring expertly crafted liquors to exploring iconic historical sites like the Acropolis in Athens, the ancient island of Delos, and medieval crusader castles. Each destination is steeped in romance and history, promising a memorable journey.[2]

Greece has a rich and influential history that dates back to ancient times, beginning with the Minoan and Mycenaean civilizations around 3000–1100 BCE. The classical period (5th–4th centuries BCE) is marked by the rise of city-states like Athens and Sparta, the birth of democracy in Athens, and the philosophical contributions of figures like Socrates, Plato, and Aristotle. After Alexander the Great's conquests in the 4th

---

1   https://worldpopulationreview.com/countries/greece

century BCE, Greek culture spread across much of the known world. Greece later fell under Roman rule and subsequently the Byzantine Empire. Following the Ottoman occupation from the 15th century to the 19th century, Greece gained independence in 1830, establishing a modern nation-state. Greece has since experienced political instability, wars, and economic challenges, yet remains a key player in both regional and global affairs.

Ancient Greece produced a remarkable array of individuals whose contributions shaped Western civilization. Philosophers like Socrates, who pioneered the Socratic method, and his student Plato, whose works laid the foundation for Western philosophy, had profound influence. Aristotle, Plato's student, made groundbreaking advancements in logic, ethics, and science. In the realm of literature, Homer's epic poems, The Iliad, and The Odyssey, are foundational texts in Western literature. In mathematics and science, figures like Pythagoras, Euclid, and Archimedes made lasting contributions to geometry, physics, and engineering. Alexander the Great, one of history's most successful military leaders, spread Greek culture across three continents, creating the Hellenistic world. Politically, Pericles was a key figure in the development of Athenian democracy, while statesmen like Themistocles and Leonidas are remembered for their leadership in the Persian Wars. These figures, among others, laid the intellectual, political, and cultural foundations for much of modern Western thought.[2]

The Capital

Athens, the capital city, is a bustling hub of economic, political, and cultural life. With over 3,000 years of recorded history, Athens is one of the world's oldest cities. Its metropolitan population of 3.8 million underscores its vital role in Europe. Athens continues to inspire, with landmarks such as the Parthenon and the influence of its patron goddess, Athena, symbolizing resilience and progress.

Athens is often regarded as the cradle of Western Civilization, particularly for its pivotal role in the development of democracy, philosophy,

---

2   https://www.thefamouspeople.com/greece.php

and the arts during the 5th century BCE. The city was the center of ancient Greek culture, home to influential figures such as Socrates, Plato, and Aristotle, and a hub of intellectual and artistic achievement. Today, Athens blends ancient history with modern life, with iconic landmarks like the Parthenon atop the Acropolis, the Temple of Olympian Zeus, and the ancient Agora standing as testaments to its rich heritage. Beyond its historical significance, Athens is a vibrant metropolis, offering a dynamic blend of cultural attractions, bustling neighborhoods, and a thriving economy. It remains a focal point for political, cultural, and economic life in Greece, continuing to influence global culture and thought.

Greece, the Basics

How to Get There?

The easiest way to get to Greece is by flying. Several airlines provide direct routes to Greece, with Singapore Airlines, Qatar Airways, and Emirates being top choices. Booking flights during the off-season (October–April) or well in advance can help secure the best prices.

When to Visit?

The best times to visit are during spring (April–June) and fall (September–October), when the weather is pleasant, and the crowds are smaller. Summer, especially July, brings hot temperatures and crowded tourist areas, but the milder months of June and September offer a good balance of warmth and comfort.

For those interested in experiencing local traditions, Orthodox Easter in April and Independence Day on March 25th are excellent opportunities to immerse in Greek culture.[3]

---

3   https://realgreekexperiences.com/
    cheapest-time-to-go-to-greece-best-times-to-visit

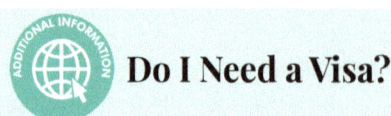

Do I Need a Visa?

Whether or not you need a visa to visit Greece depends on your nationality and the purpose of your visit.

- **EU/EEA and Swiss citizens:** Citizens of European Union (EU) countries, European Economic Area (EEA) nations, and Switzerland do not need a visa to visit Greece for short stays (up to 90 days) for tourism, business, or family visits.

- **Non-EU Citizens:**
  —Citizens from many countries, including the U.S., Canada, Australia, and New Zealand, do not require a visa for short stays (up to 90 days) for tourism or business purposes, as Greece is part of the Schengen Area. However, they must meet certain conditions, such as having a valid passport, sufficient funds for the duration of their stay, and travel insurance.
  —Citizens from other countries may need to apply for a Schengen visa before traveling. This includes most countries in Africa, Asia, and the Middle East.

- **Long-Stay Visas:** If you plan to stay in Greece for more than 90 days, you will generally need a national visa or residence permit, regardless of your nationality.

It's always a good idea to check with the Greek embassy or consulate in your country for the most current visa requirements before planning your trip.

How to Get Around

Public transportation options include buses, taxis, rental cars, ferries, and bicycles. Public buses are affordable at an average fare of €27 (US$29), and ferries provide convenient travel between islands, with prices ranging from €50 to €150 (US$54–$162). Weekly bus passes offer cost-effective solutions for extended stays.[4]

Monetary Advice

The Greek currency is Euro (€), with an exchange rate of approximately €1 to US$1.05. While credit cards are widely accepted, travelers can exchange currency at banks and airports.

Travelers arriving in Greece will find currency exchange services and ATMs conveniently located at major airports. These facilities allow visitors to exchange foreign currency for euros, the official currency of Greece. While most establishments accept credit cards, it is advisable to carry some cash for smaller purchases, tips, or emergencies.

In Greece, bargaining is common in markets and small shops, especially in tourist areas, but not in fixed-price stores. Tipping is appreciated but not mandatory. In restaurants, rounding up or leaving 5-10% is typical, while cafés and bars often see small change left. Hotel staff and taxi drivers may receive small tips, around €1–€2 (US$1.05-$2.10), and tour guides generally get €5–€10 (US$5.24-$10.48) per person for good service. Tipping is flexible and depends on the level of service.[5]

Greek Hospitality

Hospitality, or "Filoxenia," is more than just a tradition in Greece; it is a way of life deeply embedded in the cultural and historical fabric of the nation. The word *"Filoxenia"* literally translates to "friend of the stranger," reflecting an ancient ethos that regarded welcoming guests as a sacred obligation. This custom traces back to Greek mythology, where

4   https://greeking.me/blog/tips/transportation-in-greece

5   https://greeceinsiders.travel/
      how-much-does-it-cost-to-go-to-greece-budget-guide/

hospitality was considered a divine duty enforced by the gods. For instance, Zeus, the king of gods, was also referred to as *"Zeus Xenios,"* the protector of travelers and strangers.

Modern Greeks carry forward this timeless tradition with acts of kindness, generosity, and a genuine eagerness to make visitors feel at home. It is not uncommon for locals to go out of their way to assist tourists, whether by offering directions, sharing recommendations for hidden gems, or even inviting them into their homes for a meal. Such gestures often leave a lasting impression on visitors, making Greece synonymous with warmth and openness.

Cultural Etiquette and Expectations

While Greeks are naturally warm and accommodating, visitors should take care to respect the cultural norms that underpin their hospitality.[6]

- **Verbal Communication:** Greeks value clear verbal communication over nonverbal cues like nodding. A simple "yes" (*nai*) or "no" (*ochi*) is preferred to avoid misunderstandings.
- **Refusing Gifts or Invitations:** If you must decline an offer, do so with genuine gratitude and tact, as outright refusal may inadvertently cause offense.
- **Dining Etiquette:** Dining in Greece is often a communal and celebratory experience. It is customary to wait until everyone at the table has been served before beginning to eat, demonstrating respect and camaraderie. Additionally, when sharing a meal, offering compliments about the food is always appreciated.

One of the most enriching ways to experience Greek hospitality is by participating in local customs and celebrations. Festivals, or panigiria, are a cornerstone of Greek life, often held in honor of saints or historical events. These gatherings typically include music, dancing, and traditional cuisine, creating a welcoming atmosphere for locals and visitors alike.

---

6   https://www.kaliviani.com/post/
    filoxenia-the-heartbeat-of-greek-hospitality

Joining in, even as an observer, shows appreciation for the culture and fosters a sense of connection with the community.

Respecting elders is another vital aspect of Greek culture. In family settings or public interactions, showing deference to older individuals reflects good manners and an understanding of social hierarchies. Small gestures, such as greeting elders first or offering them your seat, go a long way in building goodwill.[7]

Food and drink are central to the Greek concept of hospitality. Whether in a bustling city café or a remote village taverna, the act of sharing a meal represents more than sustenance—it is a symbolic gesture of friendship and goodwill. Refusing food or drink offered by a host may unintentionally come across as impolite, so even a small taste is appreciated as a sign of respect. When dining with locals, be prepared for lively conversation, laughter, and a toast or two with a hearty *"Yamas!"* (cheers).

Greek hospitality is not just about generosity; it is about forming meaningful connections. Visitors who take the time to learn a few Greek phrases, show interest in local history, or simply smile warmly will often find their efforts reciprocated tenfold.

---

7   https://www.encounterstravel.com/blog/cultural-events-and-cele-brations-in-greece#:~:text=Some%20of%20the%20most%20im-portant%20celebrations%20in%20Greece,as%20the%20Corfu%20Carnival%20and%20the%20Epidaurus%20Festival.

CUSTOMS

CHAPTER 2
CUSTOMS

Travelers Entering Greece

Proper preparation is the cornerstone of a seamless travel experience, particularly when visiting a destination as rich in culture and history as Greece. Before embarking on their journey, travelers should ensure that all necessary documents are complete, valid, and easily accessible. This proactive approach not only helps to avoid delays or complications but also allows for a more enjoyable start to the trip.[8]

Required Documents for Entry

1. **Passport:**

   - A valid passport is essential for entry into Greece. It must remain valid for at least six months beyond the traveler's planned departure date from the country. Travelers should verify this well in advance of their trip to avoid last-minute issues.[9]

---

8   https://travel.state.gov/content/travel/en/international-travel/
    International-Travel-Country-Information-Pages/Greece.html/

9   https://www.schengenvisainfo.com/greece/visa/

2. **Visa:**

- **Short-Term Visitors:** Citizens of visa-exempt countries can stay in Greece for up to 90 days within a 180-day period without a visa.
- **Longer Stays:** For tourists intending to remain in Greece for more than 90 days, a visa is mandatory. This often applies to students, workers, or long-term visitors, and the application process should be initiated early.

3. **Travel Insurance:**

- Travelers must carry valid travel insurance that provides comprehensive coverage for medical emergencies, trip cancellations, and disruptions. Immigration authorities may request proof of this insurance during entry procedures.

4. **Proof of Accommodation:**

- Evidence of lodging arrangements is required. This can include hotel reservations, confirmation emails from booking platforms, or a letter from a host. Travelers without pre-booked accommodations may face scrutiny during immigration checks.

5. **Return Flight Ticket:**

- Visitors must present proof of a confirmed return ticket or onward travel plans to demonstrate their intention to leave Greece within the permitted time frame.

Upon landing in Greece, travelers should anticipate a thorough inspection of their documentation by immigration officers. This process includes verifying the authenticity and validity of passports, visas, and return tickets. Ensuring all documents are in order will help expedite the process and avoid unnecessary delays.

Once cleared through customs, tourists should consider their immediate transportation needs. Accessing maps and schedules for public transportation, such as buses or metro systems, can be crucial for navigating from the airport to accommodations. Many airports also offer taxi and car rental services for added convenience.

 For reliable updates and travel safety information, the "Greece International Travel Information" website is a useful resource for all tourists. **https://travel.state.gov/ content/travel/en/international-travel/International-Travel-Country-Information-Pages/Greece.html/**

Customs Entitlements and Monetary Restrictions

Greece adheres to the customs regulations set by the European Union, and travelers should familiarize themselves with these guidelines to ensure compliance.[10]

Duty-Free Allowances (for travelers from non-EU countries):

- **Tobacco:** You can bring up to 200 cigarettes, 100 cigarillos, 50 cigars, or 250 grams (8.82 ounces) of smoking tobacco.

- **Alcohol:** You are allowed to bring up to 1 liter (1.057 quarts) of spirits over 22% alcohol (e.g., whiskey, vodka), 2 liters (2.11 quarts) of fortified wine (e.g., port, sherry), or 4 liters (4.23 quarts) of still wine.

- **Perfume:** Up to 50 grams (1.76 ounces) of perfume and 250 ml (50.72 teaspoons) of eau de toilette are allowed.

- **Other Goods:** You can bring other goods for personal use with a total value not exceeding €430 (US$451) for air travelers or €300 (US$314) for other travelers. If your goods exceed these limits, customs duties may apply.

---

10 https://en.tripmydream.com/greece/custom

Personal Use Items:

- **Medicines:** You are allowed to bring personal medications for personal use, but it's a good idea to carry a prescription or doctor's note, especially for controlled substances.
- **Food:** Generally, you can bring food for personal consumption, but restrictions apply to certain items like meat, dairy products, and fresh fruit/vegetables from non-EU countries due to health and safety regulations. Items like packaged snacks, canned foods, and bottled drinks are typically allowed.

Money and Monetary Instruments

While there is no restriction on the amount of money one can bring into Greece, travelers should exercise caution when transporting large sums. Exceeding €10,000 (US$10,481) in currency or monetary instruments requires declaration at customs when leaving the country. This regulation helps prevent money laundering and other illicit activities.

If customs officers discover undeclared funds, they may temporarily confiscate the money for further investigation. Travelers found with counterfeit or stolen currency will face legal consequences. For large transactions, electronic transfers are generally safer and more secure than carrying cash.

For everyday expenses, tourists are encouraged to carry some cash in euros, as smaller businesses and rural areas may not accept credit or debit cards.[11]

 ## Restricted and Prohibited Items

When traveling to Greece, there are several restricted and prohibited items you should be aware of. These regulations are largely in line

---

11   https://www.finder.com/travel-money/greece

with EU laws since Greece is a member of the European Union. Here's a breakdown:

Restricted Items:

1. Food Products:

- **Meat and Dairy:** Importing fresh meat, dairy products, or unprocessed food from non-EU countries is restricted due to health and safety regulations. This includes items like fresh meat, milk, cheese, and eggs.
- **Fresh Fruits and Vegetables:** Certain fresh produce from non-EU countries may be restricted to prevent the spread of pests and diseases.

2. Alcohol and Tobacco:

- There are limits on the amount of alcohol and tobacco you can bring for personal use, and if you exceed these limits, you may need to pay customs duties or taxes. For example, the duty-free allowance for alcohol is 1 liter (1.057 quarts) of spirits (over 22% alcohol), or 2 liters (2.11 quarts) of fortified wine.

3. Medicines:

- You are allowed to bring personal medicines, but for controlled substances or medication containing narcotics (e.g., certain painkillers or sleeping pills), a prescription or a doctor's note is required to avoid legal complications.

4. Firearms and Ammunition:

- Firearms, ammunition, and certain weapons can be brought into Greece only with a special permit. You must declare them at customs, and they may be subject to stringent checks.

5. *Cash:*

- If you're carrying cash or monetary instruments exceeding €10,000 (US$10,481), or the equivalent in other currencies, you must declare it at customs.

Prohibited Items:

1. *Illegal Drugs:*

- The import of any form of illegal drugs (such as marijuana, cocaine, etc.) is strictly prohibited. Greece enforces strict penalties for drug trafficking and possession.

2. *Counterfeit Goods:*

- It is illegal to import or carry counterfeit items, including pirated media (CDs, DVDs), fake designer products, and knockoff electronics.

3. *Endangered Species:*

- Items made from or containing parts of endangered species are prohibited. This includes products such as ivory, certain animal skins, and products made from exotic animals. Greece follows international agreements, like CITES (Convention on International Trade in Endangered Species).

4. *Explosives, Fireworks, and Dangerous Chemicals:*

- The import of explosives, fireworks, and certain hazardous materials is strictly regulated and often prohibited, unless you have a special license.

5. *Cultural Property:*

   ▪ Exporting cultural heritage items or antiques from Greece (or other countries) is prohibited without the proper authorization. This includes ancient artifacts, historical artwork, and other culturally significant items.

6. *Plants and Plant Products:*

   ▪ There are strict regulations on bringing plants, flowers, seeds, and soil into Greece, particularly from non-EU countries, to prevent the spread of pests and diseases. Some plants may require a phytosanitary certificate.

7. *Certain Animals:*

   ▪ Bringing in certain live animals, particularly those that are endangered or pose a risk to the local ecosystem, is prohibited. Strict regulations apply to pets like dogs, cats, and birds, especially regarding vaccinations (e.g., rabies).

Other Considerations:

▪ **Pornographic Material:** Pornographic or obscene material is not permitted, and anything deemed offensive to public morality can be seized by authorities.

▪ **Banned or Controlled Medicines:** Some over-the-counter medicines available in other countries (e.g., certain painkillers, sleeping pills, or herbal remedies) may be restricted or require a prescription in Greece.

For specific details or if you're traveling with items that might fall into a gray area, it's advisable to check with Greek Customs or the Greek Embassy in your home country before your trip.

 **Five Practical Tips to Know Before You Go**

Traveling to Greece is an enriching experience, but a few practical considerations can help ensure a smooth and enjoyable journey:[12]

- **Learn Basic Greek Phrases:** While many locals in tourist areas speak English, learning simple phrases like "please" (*parakaló*) and "thank you" (*efharistó*) shows respect and can enhance your interactions.

- **Pack Light and Smart:** Greece's warm climate makes lightweight clothing ideal. However, you should include essentials like a reusable water bottle, a light jacket, and comfortable walking shoes. Exploring historical sites and rugged landscapes often involves significant walking.

- **Plan Your Itinerary in Advance:** Research and prioritize attractions you wish to visit. Greece offers a mix of historical landmarks, scenic beaches, and cultural experiences. Planning ahead will help you manage time and avoid missing key highlights.

- **Carry Extra Cash:** While credit cards are widely accepted in major cities and tourist hotspots, smaller islands and remote areas may operate on a cash-only basis. Having sufficient cash on hand is particularly important for emergencies or unexpected expenses.

- **Avoid Drinking Tap Water in Some Areas:** While tap water in major cities is generally safe to drink, it is advisable to use bottled water on smaller islands or in rural areas where water quality may vary. Always check with local sources if in doubt.

---

12   https://www.thewanderfulme.com/essential-greece-travel-tips/

CRIME IN GREECE

- Overview
- Crime Hotspots in Greece
- Crime Statistics
- Quick Safety Tips

CHAPTER 3
CRIME IN GREECE

Overview

Greece is widely regarded as one of the safest countries in Europe, making it an appealing destination for tourists. With a crime rate of 0.85 (per 100,000 people), Greece compares favorably to the United States, which has a significantly higher rate of 6.81. These figures reflect a generally low risk for visitors. However, as with any destination, exercising caution and being aware of one's surroundings is always advised.

The primary contributors to crime in Greece include organized crime and interpersonal violence. Organized crime groups are largely involved in activities such as drug trafficking, smuggling, and other illicit operations. Interpersonal crimes, though less frequent, include unlawful homicides and domestic violence and remain areas of concern within the country.

Greece's crime trends have shown fluctuations over the years, influenced by socio-economic and political factors. In recent years, crime rates have stabilized at relatively low levels after a period of higher crime in the past. While there have been occasional increases in crime in certain years, the overall trend suggests a gradual reduction and stabilization in crime over the long term. This pattern reflects a mix of factors such as improved law enforcement, economic changes, and shifting social conditions.

Crime Hotspots in Greece

In Greece, crime hotspots tend to align with certain urban areas, tourist destinations, and regions experiencing economic challenges. While overall crime rates are relatively low, certain areas are known to experience higher levels of crime, particularly related to petty theft and opportunistic offenses. **Athens**, the capital, is home to some of the most prominent hotspots. Central districts like Omonia Square and Exarchia can attract pickpockets and petty criminals, especially during the busy tourist season. Exarchia, in particular, has a reputation for political unrest, with occasional protests and clashes, while Psiri and Monastiraki can also be prone to scams and theft, given their popularity with tourists.

Further north, in **Thessaloniki**, the bustling city center and port areas face similar challenges. Although the city is generally safe, crowded locations, especially near transportation hubs, can be magnets for petty criminals. Meanwhile, Greece's famous islands, like **Mykonos** and **Santorini**, draw millions of tourists each year, which sometimes leads to an uptick in pickpocketing, particularly in the busy nightlife areas or crowded tourist attractions.

Piraeus, Athens' main port, is another area where travelers should be cautious. The terminals, teeming with people coming and going, are common spots for small thefts and scams. Lastly, in the border regions near Turkey, Albania, and North Macedonia, Greece faces occasional challenges with organized crime, particularly in smuggling and trafficking, although these areas are far from tourist destinations.

Despite these hotspots, Greece remains largely safe for both residents and visitors. Travelers are encouraged to take standard precautions, especially in crowded or tourist-heavy areas, to avoid falling victim to petty crime.

Crime Statistics

The most prevalent crimes in Greece encompass theft, smuggling, organized crime, and financial fraud. Among these, theft stands out as the most frequent, particularly in areas heavily trafficked by tourists. Smuggling and organized crime are often more sophisticated and targeted activities, typically unrelated to visitors. Financial fraud, which includes counterfeit currency and deceptive financial schemes, is also a concern but primarily affects local residents and businesses rather than tourists.

Violent crimes, such as homicides, are comparatively rare in Greece, which bolsters its reputation as one of Europe's safest travel destinations. Nonetheless, like in any country, visitors must remain cautious to avoid becoming victims of opportunistic crimes.[13]

Quick Safety Tips

Although no location is entirely without risk, Greece's well-organized law enforcement and community-oriented culture contribute to a secure environment for visitors. Tourists can take proactive steps to ensure a safe and enjoyable experience in Greece:[14]

1. **Stay Alert:** Be aware of your surroundings, especially in crowded areas like markets and tourist sites. Avoid displaying valuables to prevent attracting attention.

2. **Protect Your Belongings:** Use anti-theft bags and never leave valuables unattended. Keep essentials with you and store larger items in a hotel safe.

3. **Avoid Scams:** Be cautious of overly friendly strangers or unsolicited offers. Stick to licensed services and decline suspicious requests.

---

13 https://www.ncesc.com/geographic-faq/what-is-the-main-crime-in-greece/#:~:text=The%20most%20widespread%20crimes%20to%20affect%20Greece%20are,particularly%20works%20of%20art%20%E2%80%93%20and%20financial%20crime.

14 https://www.worldnomads.com/travel-safety/europe/greece/petty-crime-in-greece

4. **Avoid Protests:** Stay clear of protests, which can escalate quickly. If near one, find a safe place and stay informed about local events.

5. **Prepare for Natural Disasters:** Familiarize yourself with emergency procedures for earthquakes and wildfires. Stay updated on local news and alerts.

CRIMINAL LAW VIOLATIONS

CHAPTER 4

CRIMINAL LAW VIOLATIONS

Marijuana and Other Drugs in Greece

Marijuana has a historical and cultural connection to Greece, with evidence suggesting its use dates back to ancient times. Stories and myths from Greek history reference cannabis, and the word itself originates from the Greek verb *cannabeizein*, meaning "to smoke cannabis." Historically, Greece was a major exporter of marijuana across Europe until its prohibition in 1890.

Today, the legal landscape has evolved significantly. Recreational marijuana use is illegal, and medical marijuana is allowed under strict regulations. Following a 1987 policy shift, Greece began treating drug addicts as patients rather than criminals. This change reclassified marijuana from a Schedule A (high-risk) drug to Schedule B, permitting its medicinal use.

Greek citizens with a valid medical marijuana card and a physician's prescription may obtain cannabis with a THC content of no more than 0.2%. Physicians in Greece are reportedly more inclined to prescribe medical marijuana for conditions like depression, favoring its therapeutic effects over traditional antidepressants.

However, the recreational use, possession, and/or trafficking of marijuana remains strictly prohibited. The stringent drug laws reflect Greece's effort to balance medical needs with public safety, focusing on regulated medicinal cannabis while combating overconsumption and illegal trafficking.[15]

In Greece, drug laws are strict, with a zero-tolerance approach to the use, possession, and trafficking of illicit substances. Possessing even small amounts of illegal drugs like heroin or cocaine can lead to fines, detention, or imprisonment, and there is no distinction between personal use and possession. Drug trafficking is severely punished, often with long prison sentences. Driving under the influence of drugs is a criminal offense, and individuals caught may face fines, bans, and imprisonment. Greece adheres to international drug control agreements, ensuring robust enforcement of its drug laws. Travelers should be cautious, as even small quantities of drugs can lead to significant legal consequences.

Prescription Medication

When traveling to Greece with prescription medications, it's important to follow the country's legal requirements. Travelers can bring up to five types of prescribed medications for personal use, with a maximum of two boxes per type. Medications must be in their original packaging with the prescription label clearly showing the traveler's name. It's also recommended to carry a letter from your healthcare provider outlining the medications, dosage, and conditions being treated, as this may be required by customs or medical personnel.

For transportation, medications can be carried in both carry-on and checked baggage, with no specific quantity limits, but liquids exceeding 3.4 ounces must be declared at security. It's best to pack essential medications in carry-on luggage for easy access, especially considering time zone changes that may affect medication schedules.

Additionally, travelers should check whether their medications are legal in Greece, as some drugs available over the counter in other countries may be controlled. Bringing enough medication for the entire trip, plus extra in case of delays, is also recommended. Finally, staying informed

---

15   https://amsterdammarijuanaseeds.com/blog/greece-cannabis-laws/

about local health advisories and seeking travel-specific medical advice can help ensure a safe and smooth journey.[16]

Penalties

In Greece, penalties for drug-related offenses are severe, reflecting the country's strict stance on illicit drugs. The legal framework for drug crimes includes the possession, trafficking, production, and use of illegal substances, with varying penalties depending on the offense's nature and severity:

- **Possession of Illicit Drugs:** Even possessing small amounts of illegal drugs, such as marijuana, heroin, or cocaine, for personal use can lead to serious legal consequences. Penalties may include fines, detention, or imprisonment. The severity depends on the type and amount of the drug. Larger quantities or repeat offenses can result in longer prison sentences. Additionally, possessing prescription drugs without a valid prescription is also illegal and can lead to fines or imprisonment.

- **Drug Trafficking and Distribution:** Drug trafficking is met with severe penalties, including long prison sentences, typically 10 years or more. This depends on factors like the type and quantity of the drug, as well as involvement in organized crime. Similarly, those involved in the production or manufacturing of drugs face harsh punishments, with lengthy prison terms and significant fines, similar to those given to traffickers.

- **Drug Use and Driving:** Using drugs and driving is a serious offense. Penalties for driving under the influence of drugs can include fines, a driving ban, and imprisonment, depending on the severity of the offense.

- **Cultivation of Drugs:** Growing or cultivating illegal drugs, such as marijuana, is also illegal in Greece and can result in severe penalties, including imprisonment.

---

16   https://www.which.co.uk/reviews/travel-health/article/
how-to-travel-with-your-medication-legally-and-safely-aBT8I3o3iWIw

- **Drug Smuggling:** Being involved in drug smuggling, particularly at the international level, can result in life sentences and severe fines. Greece's strategic location in the Mediterranean means that it is often a target for international drug trafficking routes, and the penalties reflect the seriousness of these offenses.

- **Possession with Intent to Distribute:** Those found with large quantities of drugs, suggesting an intent to distribute, face severe sentences similar to those for trafficking, even if they have not yet engaged in distribution.

 **General Questions**

1. *Is cannabis legal in Greece?* No. Cannabis is illegal for recreational use in Greece. The country enforces stringent laws against its possession, use, or distribution for non-medical purposes. However, medical marijuana is permitted under highly regulated circumstances. Only Greek citizens with a certified medical condition, a valid medical marijuana card, and a physician's prescription may legally obtain and use cannabis for medicinal purposes. **Tourists or foreign visitors are not eligible to partake in Greece's medical marijuana program.**

2. *Where can I legally purchase marijuana in Greece?* Medical marijuana is available exclusively to individuals with a valid prescription and medical marijuana card, and it can only be purchased at licensed pharmacies or authorized dispensaries. These facilities operate under strict oversight from the Greek government to ensure that the product is used solely for its intended medical purposes. The purchasing process is monitored closely, with the requirement of presenting both the medical card and the prescription at the time of purchase.

   Recreational cannabis is not legally available for sale anywhere in Greece, and attempting to purchase or possess it can lead to legal repercussions.

3. *Can I have marijuana on my person or in my hotel room in Greece?* **No.** Tourists are not allowed to possess marijuana in Greece under any circumstances, even if they hold a medical prescription or card issued in their home country. This restriction applies to carrying cannabis on one's person, storing it in accommodations such as hotels, or transporting it within Greece.

   Even small amounts of cannabis, if found in the possession of a tourist, can lead to penalties ranging from fines to criminal charges. Greek authorities have a zero-tolerance policy for non-compliance with their drug laws, making it essential for visitors to avoid carrying or using marijuana during their stay.

4. *Are there any exceptions for tourists?* **No exceptions** exist for tourists regarding the possession, purchase, or use of cannabis in Greece. While Greek citizens with the appropriate documentation may access medical marijuana, these legal protections do not extend to foreign visitors.

   Even tourists who use medical marijuana in their home countries must adhere to Greece's laws, which prohibit importing or using cannabis, regardless of the purpose. Tourists with medical needs are advised to explore alternative, legally permitted medications before traveling to Greece.

5. *What are the penalties for possessing and consuming other types of illicit drugs in Greece?* Greece enforces strict penalties for the possession, use, or trafficking of illicit drugs, including those beyond cannabis. Penalties for drug-related offenses vary based on the offense. Possession of even small amounts of drugs can result in imprisonment for up to five years, with fines ranging from €200 to €2,000 (US$210 to $2,096). Trafficking or distributing drugs like cocaine, LSD, or synthetic marijuana carries severe penalties, including prison sentences of eight years or more, along with hefty fines ranging from €50,000 to €1,000,000 (US$52,453 to $1,049,050). Foreign nationals caught committing drug-related offenses may also face expulsion from the country. Greece enforces uniform penalties for all controlled substances, regardless of the drug type.[17]

 **Law of the Land Hypothetical**

HYPOTHETICAL: *A tourist prescribed SSRIs (antidepressants) for depression plans a week-long visit to Greece and needs to bring 14 pills. While these medications are allowed, the tourist also uses CBD oil for anxiety. Can a tourist bring CBD oil to Greece for personal use if they are also bringing prescribed medication?"*

ANSWER: **No.** *The CBD oil must be left behind. Despite its therapeutic use and legal status in some countries, CBD oil derived from cannabis is prohibited for tourists in Greece. Instead, the traveler should rely on their other prescribed medications and consult a healthcare provider for alternative solutions during the trip.*

---

17 https://www.drugpolicyfacts.org/region/greece

 **Takeaways**

- Marijuana is illegal for recreational use in Greece, and medical marijuana is only available to Greek citizens with a prescription. Tourists cannot possess or use cannabis, even for medical purposes.

- Possessing illegal drugs, even in small amounts, can result in fines, imprisonment, or both. Drug trafficking and smuggling carry long prison sentences and hefty fines.

- Travelers can bring prescribed medications but must carry them in their original packaging with a valid prescription. Some medications may be regulated in Greece.

- Tourists are not allowed to possess or use cannabis, even if prescribed in their home country. They should consult a doctor for alternatives.

- Foreigners caught with drugs may face fines, jail time, and expulsion from Greece. Tourists should be mindful of strict drug laws.

CHAPTER 5

ALCOHOL-RELATED OFFENSES

IN THIS CHAPTER

- Alcohol-Related Offenses
- Alcohol Regulation
- Things to Remember
- General Questions
- Law of the Land Hypothetical
- Takeaways

CHAPTER 5

ALCOHOL-RELATED OFFENSES

Alcohol-Related Offenses

Alcohol has long held a significant place in Greek history and culture. Ancient Greeks regarded alcohol, particularly wine, as a sacred substance, often used in offerings to the gods for fortune and luck. Dionysus, the deity of wine and revelry, symbolizes the cultural importance of alcohol in ancient Greece.

Beer, Greece's first major alcoholic product, laid the foundation for the thriving wine industry that followed. By around 4000 BCE, Greece had established itself as a prominent exporter of wine throughout Europe, solidifying alcohol's role as both a cultural and economic cornerstone.

In modern Greece, alcohol remains a vital aspect of social life. It is enjoyed during holidays, celebrations, and daily interactions, often as a communal activity. While alcohol is widely consumed, most Greeks demonstrate responsible drinking habits, emphasizing moderation and social connection.

Several iconic drinks are closely associated with Greek culture:

- **Wine:** A historic staple of Greek celebrations.
- **Ouzo:** An anise-flavored aperitif, often paired with meze (small dishes).

- **Raki:** A strong, clear spirit enjoyed across Crete and other regions.
- **Retsina:** A unique wine infused with pine resin.
- **Tsipouro:** A potent distilled spirit.
- **Metaxa Brandy:** A smooth, aromatic liquor with a rich heritage.

While alcohol is legal and widely available in Greece, certain behaviors and offenses, such as underage drinking and drunk driving, are regulated to ensure public safety and cultural respect.[18]

Alcohol Regulation

In Greece, alcohol regulations are designed to balance enjoyment with public safety, with a particular focus on protecting minors and maintaining responsible consumption. The minimum legal drinking age is set at 18, and this applies to both purchasing and consuming alcohol in public spaces. While establishments like bars, restaurants, and clubs may request identification from anyone who appears under 18, this practice is not always uniformly enforced, especially in more relaxed settings or smaller venues.

Alcohol advertising is tightly regulated, with specific restrictions in place to prevent the promotion of alcoholic beverages to minors. This includes prohibitions on ads that appeal to children or teenagers, ensuring that alcohol marketing focuses on adult audiences only. Additionally, alcohol consumption is largely accepted in social contexts, such as meals and gatherings, reflecting Greece's rich cultural ties to wine, ouzo, and other traditional drinks.

Law enforcement plays a significant role in ensuring compliance with alcohol laws. The Hellenic Police actively monitor the enforcement of the legal drinking age, and penalties for violations, particularly those involving minors, can include fines for establishments or individuals caught breaking the rules. One of the most critical areas of alcohol regulation

---

18   https://www.alcoholproblemsandsolutions.org/
     alcohol-in-antiquity-ancient-greeks/

is the enforcement of laws against drunk driving. Greece has strict DUI (driving under the influence) laws, and penalties for violations can include hefty fines, license suspension, and even imprisonment, depending on the severity of the offense.

Overall, while alcohol is an integral part of Greek culture and social life, the country takes a responsible approach to its consumption, particularly when it comes to protecting young people and ensuring public safety on the roads.[19]

 **Things to Remember**

- **Drinking Age:** The legal drinking age in Greece is 18 years old.

- **Public Consumption:** It is generally legal to drink alcohol in public spaces, including the streets, and carry an open container, though local regulations may vary, with some municipalities imposing restrictions in specific areas like tourist zones or during certain times.

- **Public Drunkenness:** public drunkenness itself is not typically a criminal offense, but it can lead to fines or arrest if the individual's behavior becomes disruptive or poses a risk to public safety. Violations like disturbing the peace, aggressive behavior, or creating a disturbance while intoxicated can result in penalties, including fines or detention. Additionally, if public drunkenness leads to other infractions, such as disorderly conduct or impaired driving, more severe legal consequences may apply.

- **Drunk Driving:** The legal BAC limit for drivers is 0.5 g/L, with a €200 (US$210) fine for exceeding it. Higher BAC levels (1.10 g/L or more) result in severe penalties, including prison sentences starting at two months. Tourists are advised to avoid driving after drinking due to strict laws and serious consequences.

---

19 https://www.hinterlandtravel.com/greece/customs

- **Purchasing Alcohol:** There are few restrictions on purchasing alcohol, but the legal drinking age is 18. Alcohol can be bought from supermarkets, liquor stores, and licensed establishments like bars and restaurants. However, sales are prohibited to minors, and some municipalities may impose additional regulations, such as limiting alcohol sales during certain hours or in specific areas, especially near schools or in tourist zones.

- **Illegal Alcohol:** Illegal alcohol is an issue in Greece, particularly in some tourist areas, where counterfeit or unlicensed alcohol may be sold at lower prices. This "bootleg" alcohol can pose serious health risks, including poisoning, and is subject to legal penalties for both sellers and consumers. Authorities actively work to combat the distribution of illegal alcohol, but it remains a concern, especially in less regulated markets.

 **General Questions**

1. *Can I drink and drive in Greece?* **No.** It is illegal to drink and drive in Greece. While enforcement can be lenient in certain cases, penalties for exceeding the BAC limit range from fines to imprisonment, depending on the severity of the violation.

2. *Can I possess an open container in public?* **Yes.** Open containers of alcohol are permitted in public spaces. However, tourists should consume alcohol responsibly to avoid offending locals or attracting unnecessary attention.

 **Law of the Land Hypothetical**

HYPOTHETICAL: *I am a tourist at a restaurant enjoying a drink. As I get my drink topped off without finishing the previous serving, I notice others giving me disapproving looks. What is the drink etiquette in Greece?*

ANSWER: *In Greece, drinking is deeply embedded in social norms that emphasize moderation and etiquette. Topping off a drink before finishing it is considered impolite, as it implies a disregard for the communal and mindful nature of drinking. To avoid offending locals, tourists should follow local customs and consume alcohol thoughtfully.*

 **Takeaways**

- Alcohol is an integral part of Greek history and daily life, celebrated for its communal and social aspects.

- Tourists are encouraged to drink responsibly and respect local customs to ensure a positive experience.

- Greece enforces strict regulations on drunk driving, with penalties ranging from fines to imprisonment for high BAC levels.

- While public consumption of alcohol is legal, maintaining decorum and avoiding excessive intoxication are key to fostering goodwill with locals.

FIREARM & AMMUNITION OFFENSES

CHAPTER 6
FIREARM & AMMUNITION OFFENSES

Current Firearm Status

In Greece, firearms are strictly regulated, and only individuals who are 18 years or older, hold a valid permit, and have their weapon registered with the Hellenic Police may legally possess a gun. As long as the firearm is registered and legally owned, there are no limits on the number of firearms a person can own. However, the law prohibits the use of automatic weapons, allowing firearms solely for self-defense, hunting, and sport shooting.

Those wishing to own a firearm must pass several rigorous screenings, including a background check and mental health evaluation, with the police conducting a thorough investigation. Additionally, gun owners are required to store their weapons safely, ensuring that they are kept out of reach of children and minors.

While there are no additional restrictions on carrying firearms in public, they must be kept with the safety on and cannot be fully loaded. The same regulations that apply to purchasing and owning a firearm also govern its public possession.[20]

---

20 https://www.buffalorifles.org/blog/are-guns-legal-in-greece/

Traveling to Greece with a firearm requires strict adherence to legal regulations. Only smooth bore shotguns are allowed for importation, and even then, travelers must obtain special permission from Greek authorities. Handguns and rifles are generally prohibited for personal import. To bring a firearm into Greece, travelers need proper documentation, such as a weapons license or European firearms passport, and must comply with importation procedures.

Travelers considering bringing firearms to Greece should fully comprehend the potential consequences of non-compliance with local regulations. Although cultural practices in regions like Crete may allow locals to use firearms with fewer restrictions, these customs do not apply to tourists, making it crucial for visitors to follow national laws. Possession of a firearm without the requisite permits can lead to criminal charges, confiscation of the weapon, and even deportation from the country.[21] Greek authorities take violations of firearm laws very seriously, and tourists may find navigating the legal system daunting if they are subject to legal action.

 **Penalties[22]**

Possession of Illegal Firearms

Individuals found in unlawful possession of firearms in Greece face serious legal consequences, including arrest, a fine of up to **US$10,000**, and imprisonment for up to five years. If the illegal firearm is used in the commission of a crime, the individual could face a sentence of up to 20 years in prison. These strict penalties serve to deter the possession and use of unregistered firearms and ensure public safety.

---

21 https://www.m1911.org/gun_laws.htm

22 https://www.buffalorifles.org/blog/are-guns-legal-in-greece/

Trafficking and Smuggling Firearms

Individuals caught involved in firearm trafficking or smuggling can face long prison sentences, substantial fines, and even additional charges if organized crime is involved. The exact penalties vary depending on the specifics of the case, such as the type and number of firearms, the scale of the trafficking operation, and whether there is evidence of criminal organization involvement. Convictions can lead to imprisonment for several years, along with hefty financial penalties.

Firearm Use in Crimes

Using a firearm in the commission of a crime results in severe penalties, including long prison sentences and substantial fines. The penalties vary depending on the severity of the crime, such as assault, robbery, or murder, with sentences often extending from several years to life. If the firearm used is unlicensed or illegally possessed, additional charges and harsher penalties apply. Aggravating factors, such as involvement in organized crime or the use of firearms in particularly violent acts, can lead to even more severe consequences.

Unauthorized Carrying of Firearms

In Greece, carrying a firearm without proper authorization is a serious offense with severe penalties. Those caught in possession of an unlicensed firearm typically face imprisonment for 1 to 5 years, along with significant fines. The firearm will also be confiscated. If the unauthorized weapon is used in a crime or if multiple firearms are involved, the penalties are even harsher, including longer prison sentences and higher fines.

Organized Crime Involvement

The use of firearms in organized crime is treated as a particularly serious offense in Greece, and the penalties are severe. Individuals found using firearms in connection with organized criminal activities face prison sentences ranging from 10 years to life, depending on the nature of the crime and the involvement in the organization. Offenders may also face additional charges related to their involvement in organized crime, such as conspiracy, trafficking, or violent crime, which can lead to more severe penalties. In addition, there may be significant financial penalties imposed alongside imprisonment, particularly if the crime involves large-scale trafficking or illegal operations. Any assets or property obtained through criminal activities may be seized by authorities.

Juvenile Firearm Offenses

Penalties for juveniles using firearms focus on rehabilitation rather than harsh punishment. Depending on the offense, juveniles may face imprisonment for up to 5 years, detention in juvenile centers, or alternative measures like probation or community service. In more severe cases, the parents or guardians could be held responsible. The legal system emphasizes correction and education, with serious offenses treated more severely.

 **General Questions**

1. *What happens if the police catch me carrying a firearm in Greece?* If the police catch you carrying a firearm as a tourist in Greece, you could face severe legal consequences. The authorities will likely confiscate the firearm, and you could be charged with illegal possession, leading to penalties such as fines, imprisonment, or both. In some cases, tourists may also face deportation, depending on the severity of the offense.

2. *What is the potential sentence for a firearms violation upon conviction?* The potential prison sentence can range from 5 years to 20 years depending on what occurred while the tourist was in possession of the firearm.

 **Law of the Land True Story**

In a major operation in Athens, Greek police seized a large cache of explosives and firearms, dismantling a significant criminal weapons distribution network. The raids, which took place across five locations, led to the arrest of five individuals. Authorities uncovered 60 kilograms of ammonium dynamite, military-grade explosives, detonators, and fuse cords, as well as assault rifles, handguns, nearly 6,000 rounds of ammunition, gold coins, and over €23,000 euros in cash. These raids follow recent terrorism-related arrests linked to a deadly bombing in Athens, although police have not confirmed whether the explosives were purchased through criminal networks.[23]

 **Takeaways**

- In Greece, only those over 18 with a valid permit can legally own firearms. Ownership requires background checks, mental health evaluations, and secure storage. Automatic weapons are banned, and firearms are restricted to self-defense, hunting, and sport shooting.

- Unauthorized possession of firearms in Greece can result in fines up to US$10,000 and prison sentences up to five years. Using

---

23 https://apnews.com/article/police-arms-seizure-greece-explosives-crime-3adb3ab5bd57f352da446d862c4b833a

firearms in crimes or trafficking can lead to harsher penalties, including long prison sentences and financial fines.

- Tourists can only bring smooth bore shotguns into Greece with special permission. They must provide proper documentation, and failure to comply can result in criminal charges, confiscation of the weapon, and deportation.

CHAPTER 7

PROSTITUTION

IN THIS CHAPTER

- Overview
- Laws and Penalties
- Prostitution Practices
- Sex Trafficking and Exploitation
- Sex Tourism and Public Health
- Tips to Avoid Being Solicited
- Law of the Land Hypothetical
- Takeaways

PROSTITUTION

Overview

Prostitution in Greece is legal, but it is regulated under specific laws designed to manage and control the industry. The primary legal framework governing prostitution in Greece is the **Law 2734/1999**, which permits the practice under certain conditions, such as being registered with the authorities and working in licensed brothels. **Sex workers must be over the age of 18** and must undergo regular health checks for sexually transmitted diseases, ensuring their safety and the safety of clients.

While prostitution is legal in regulated environments, street prostitution and soliciting sex in public places are illegal. It is also prohibited for third parties, such as pimps or traffickers, to profit from sex work or exploit workers. These activities are subject to criminal penalties, including imprisonment.

Tourism, especially in cities like Athens and Thessaloniki, and areas like Mykonos, plays a role in the local sex industry, as some visitors seek out these services. However, Greece has a relatively strong system for monitoring the industry and preventing exploitation, including human trafficking.

Despite the legal framework, issues such as human trafficking and the exploitation of vulnerable individuals, including minors, are ongoing challenges. The Greek government, along with non-governmental organizations (NGOs), has implemented initiatives to combat these problems, but challenges remain in ensuring that all sex workers are protected and not coerced into their profession. Legal support and services are available for individuals who may wish to leave sex work or seek assistance, although some individuals remain at risk due to economic vulnerability.

 **Laws and Penalties**

While prostitution in Greece is legal under specific regulations, engaging in sex work outside these legal boundaries can lead to criminal charges. The Greek Penal Code outlines various offenses related to sex work, including procuring, trafficking, exploitation, and soliciting in public places. While working as a sex worker in a licensed and regulated brothel is legal, street prostitution or soliciting in public is prohibited, and those found guilty may face fines or imprisonment.

Procuring someone to engage in prostitution, living off the earnings of prostitution, or trafficking individuals for sexual exploitation are serious criminal offenses, with penalties that can include imprisonment for several years. Those involved in human trafficking or organizing illegal prostitution rings face the harshest penalties, which can extend up to 20 years in prison.

Tourists engaging in sex work in Greece may also face penalties if they violate local laws, especially if they participate in unregulated prostitution or soliciting in public spaces. Greek authorities have the right to fine or deport individuals believed to be engaging in sex work or trafficking activities. Furthermore, individuals involved in illegal activities like pimping or sex trafficking may be subject to legal action, including imprisonment and significant fines.

Prostitution Practices

Most sex workers in Greece work in licensed **brothels** that meet specific health and safety standards. These establishments are predominantly located in major cities, where tourists and locals alike may seek their services. Many of these workers are local women, though there are also foreign nationals involved in sex work, often under less favorable conditions, with some facing exploitation or trafficking.

While brothels are regulated, **street prostitution**, which is visible in certain parts of Athens, is illegal. Street-based sex workers may solicit clients in specific areas, typically near nightclubs, busy streets, or tourist hotspots. These women often face greater risks of exploitation and violence compared to those working in regulated environments. Additionally, **massage parlors** and **private apartments** may sometimes act as fronts for illegal prostitution or brothels, especially in tourist-heavy areas like Mykonos and Santorini.

Gay prostitution, while less visible, also exists in Greece, though it tends to be discreet, often centered around specific bars, clubs, or private locations. As in many countries, there is a stigma attached to male sex work, but there has been growing acceptance of LGBTQ+ rights in recent years.

Despite being legal in certain forms, sex work in Greece faces a mix of regulation, tolerance, and selective enforcement. While prostitution may be a visible part of the local economy in tourist areas, authorities do take action against illegal activities, such as human trafficking and unlicensed brothels, which are subject to legal penalties.

Sex Trafficking and Exploitation

Sex trafficking and exploitation are serious issues in Greece, with the country being both a source and destination for trafficking victims, largely due to its significant role as a tourist hub and its location as a point of entry into the European Union. Vulnerabilities arising from economic hardship, poverty, and social inequalities contribute to Greece's trafficking problem, with women, children, and migrant workers being the most targeted groups. Victims of trafficking are often coerced or deceived into exploitative situations, lured by false promises of work in the tourism or hospitality industries, only to find themselves trapped in sexual exploitation.

Tourist-heavy areas, such as Athens, Mykonos, and Thessaloniki, have been identified as locations where trafficked individuals may be forced into prostitution, both in licensed brothels and in illegal street-based sex work. Additionally, Greece's significant migrant population, particularly from Eastern Europe, Africa, and the Middle East, makes individuals from these regions particularly vulnerable to trafficking networks that exploit their precarious legal and economic status.

The Greek government has taken various measures to address sex trafficking and exploitation. The country has ratified the European Convention on Action Against Trafficking in Human Beings and established the National Center for the Social Support of Victims of Trafficking, which provides shelter, psychological support, and legal aid to trafficking victims. Greece is also part of the European Union's anti-trafficking initiatives, working alongside international organizations such as Interpol and the U.S. State Department to combat trafficking networks. The police have had some success in raiding illegal brothels and dismantling trafficking rings, but challenges remain, particularly with addressing the root causes of trafficking, such as economic disparities and insufficient victim support services.

While the Greek government has made strides in combating trafficking, there are still significant gaps in victim protection and resources for law enforcement. Corruption, underreporting, and a lack of comprehensive victim rehabilitation systems continue to impede effective action. Vulnerable groups, including migrants and minors, remain at high risk, with cases of child sex trafficking and exploitation being reported, particularly within the illegal sex trade industry. Despite these ongoing issues, Greece is taking steps to improve public awareness, enhance law enforcement training, and collaborate internationally to tackle trafficking, but the problem persists as a major challenge.

 ## Sex Tourism and Public Health

Sex tourism in Greece, while not openly promoted, is an ongoing issue in certain tourist-heavy areas, particularly those known for their vibrant nightlife and beach resorts. Popular destinations such as Athens, Mykonos, Thessaloniki, and parts of Crete see a higher incidence of sex tourism, which tends to be linked to the influx of international visitors seeking both leisure and adult entertainment. Mykonos, for example, is well known for its luxury tourism and thriving party scene, which attracts tourists from all over the world, some of whom may seek out sex tourism services. In Athens, with its mix of historical appeal and bustling nightlife, there is also a notable presence of sex tourism, often in more discreet settings like private apartments, bars, and nightclubs. The demand for sex tourism in these regions is often facilitated by informal networks, word of mouth, and connections with local service providers, such as taxi drivers, hotel staff, and nightlife venues.

Sex tourism in Greece is a grey area; it operates in the informal economy, with sex workers often providing services in hidden or private settings. Some may advertise through online platforms, classified ads, or via personal contacts. The industry is often linked to human trafficking, with vulnerable individuals from both within Greece and from other countries being exploited. Despite government efforts to curb sex tourism, including police raids on illegal brothels and increased scrutiny on businesses that facilitate such activities, the issue persists, particularly in areas with a high concentration of tourists.

Sex tourism in Greece also presents significant public health risks, particularly in relation to the transmission of sexually transmitted infections (STIs), including HIV. The high volume of tourists seeking sex services increases the risk of STI exposure, both among sex workers and clients. Many sex workers, particularly those in the informal sector, often lack access to health services, education on safe sexual practices, and adequate protection, leading to a greater chance of unsafe sexual activity and the spread of infections. While there have been public health initiatives to provide education, condom distribution, and STI testing, gaps remain, particularly for street-based or non-formal sex workers.

These workers may be less likely to access health resources, and their lack of protection exacerbates the spread of STIs within both the tourist population and the local community. The government, along with NGOs, continues to tackle these health risks, but the hidden and often stigmatized nature of the sex tourism industry poses ongoing challenges in controlling the spread of infections.

 **Tips to Avoid Being Solicited**

To avoid being solicited by sex workers while traveling in Greece, consider these practical tips:

- **Choose reputable accommodations:** Stay in well-known, reputable areas such as high-quality hotels or resorts, particularly those located in main tourist zones. Avoid accommodations in areas with a known history of illegal activity, especially in more remote or less populated neighborhoods.

- **Avoid engaging in unwanted interactions:** If approached by someone soliciting sex, remain polite but firm. Politely decline and move on. Do not engage in any conversation that could be misinterpreted as interest.

- **Stay in busy, well-lit areas:** Stick to tourist-friendly areas that are populated and well-lit, particularly at night. Avoid walking alone in isolated or poorly lit streets, especially late at night.

- **Be cautious of certain establishments:** Avoid bars, nightclubs, or massage parlors that seem to attract tourists and may have a reputation for being linked to the sex industry. If you're unsure about a venue, do some research or ask locals for advice.

- **Understand the legal risks:** Prostitution is illegal in Greece outside certain regulated areas. Engaging in such activities can result in legal consequences, including fines or arrest. Always stick to legal and regulated activities while in the country.

 ## Law of the Land Hypothetical

HYPOTHETICAL: *Jim and Mary are on vacation in Greece and engage in paid sexual encounters with local sex workers during their stay in Mykonos. Is their behavior legal in Greece?*

ANSWER: *While prostitution itself is not illegal in Greece, it is regulated and must occur within licensed brothels or in specific areas designated for sex work. If Jim and Mary engage in paid sexual encounters with individuals outside of these regulated spaces, they could be breaking the law. Additionally, the sex workers involved may be subject to legal restrictions, depending on their employment status. If their activities are found to involve any form of exploitation, trafficking, or coercion, they could face more serious legal consequences. Furthermore, if Jim and Mary's actions are tied to sex tourism or illegal activities, such as hiring underage workers or engaging in human trafficking, they could face criminal charges, especially if the incidents are reported to local authorities. It's also worth noting that some countries have extraterritorial laws against sex tourism, which could impact Jim and Mary upon their return home.*

 ## Takeaways

- Prostitution is legal in Greece if workers are registered and operate in licensed brothels or designated zones. Soliciting outside these areas is illegal.

- Violations, such as engaging in unlicensed prostitution or trafficking, carry serious penalties, including fines and imprisonment.

- Greece faces significant issues with sex trafficking, particularly involving vulnerable migrants. Efforts to combat trafficking continue but challenges remain.

- Sex tourism is legal in Greece, with health checks required for workers. Tourists should use licensed services to avoid legal or exploitation risks.

CHAPTER 8
LGBTQ

CHAPTER 8

LGBTQ

Homophobia in Greece

Ancient Greece has long been recognized for its acceptance and cele-bration of same-sex relationships, a progressive stance that was evident in its myths, legends, and cultural practices. The works of philosophers such as Aristotle also reflect this open attitude toward same-sex love and relationships, with numerous historical accounts pointing to the prominence of queer elements in Greek society. This period marked a time when Greek culture was notably inclusive of diverse sexualities and gender identities, positioning the ancient Greeks as ahead of their time in terms of LGBTQ+ acceptance.

However, this progressive outlook underwent a significant shift with the rise of Alexander the Great's reign and the introduction of Christianity. As the political landscape changed and new religious beliefs took hold, attitudes toward LGBTQ+ individuals became less favorable. The influ-ence of Christianity, which historically viewed same-sex relationships as sinful, led to the marginalization and discrimination of the LGBTQ+ community for centuries, resulting in periods of severe social and legal challenges.

In more recent times, however, Greece has made notable strides toward inclusivity and equality. After years of social and legal discrimination, same-sex marriage was legalized in Greece in 2017, with the law being officially implemented in 2018. This legislation marked a significant step forward in recognizing the rights of LGBTQ+ individuals, allowing them to marry legally and participate fully in society. Although Greece's journey toward LGBTQ+ equality has been complex and at times challenging, these developments highlight the country's ongoing efforts to create a more inclusive and accepting environment for all citizens.[24]

Recent Trends

In Greece, major urban areas such as Athens, Mykonos, and Thessaloniki tend to be more inclusive and supportive of LGBTQ+ individuals, providing environments that encourage self-expression and cultural acceptance. Conversely, smaller, rural regions—often shaped by the conservative teachings of the Greek Orthodox Church—exhibit lower levels of acceptance, leading to heightened challenges for LGBTQ+ individuals in these locales. The contrasting dynamics reflect a society in transition, navigating the interplay between progressive legal frameworks and deeply rooted traditional beliefs.

Despite the landmark legalization of same-sex marriage in 2024 following the passage of Marriage Equality Bill in Parliament, the LGBTQ+ community in Greece continues to encounter discrimination, especially outside metropolitan hubs. Issues related to employment, education, and family life remain significant hurdles for many, compounded by fears that law enforcement entities inadequately respond to hate crimes. This pervasive concern has fostered a lack of trust in authorities among LGBTQ+ individuals, emphasizing the pressing need for more robust legal protections and responsive measures to guarantee the safety and equal rights of all citizens.

Penalties

In Greece, LGBTQ+ individuals are not subject to legal penalties, and the country has made notable progress in recognizing their rights. Homosexuality was decriminalized in 1951, and in 2015, Greece introduced a civil union law that allows same-sex couples to enjoy many of

---

24   https://www.greeklish.net/lgbt-in-greek-history/#lgbt-rights-in-greece

the same legal protections as married heterosexual couples. In February 2024, same-sex marriage was legalized.

Discrimination based on sexual orientation and gender identity is prohibited under Greek law, and hate speech and hate crimes targeting LGBTQ+ individuals are criminalized. In 2017, Greece also passed a law allowing individuals to legally change their gender without requiring surgery or psychological evaluation, marking a significant improvement in trans rights. Today, members of the LGBTQ+ community in Greece enjoy greater freedoms to express their identities, enter into legally recognized marriages, and access family-building options such as adoption or assisted reproductive technologies like IVF. However, it is important to note that while the country has made significant strides, the level of acceptance varies by region.[25]

LGBTQ Tourism and Safety Concerns

Greece stands out as an attractive and welcoming destination for members of the LGBTQ+ community, offering a diverse range of experiences tailored to LGBTQ+ travelers. With its array of gay-friendly beaches, resorts, and activities, as well as specialized LGBTQ+ tours, the country provides a rich and inclusive environment for queer individuals and couples. In fact, Greece has earned a reputation as one of the most popular LGBTQ destinations.

The most LGBTQ-friendly locations in Greece include Athens, Mykonos, and Lesbos. These cities are known for their open-mindedness and acceptance, providing numerous spaces for LGBTQ+ people to express themselves freely. **Mykonos**, in particular, is renowned for its thriving LGBTQ+ scene, drawing visitors seeking a mix of relaxation and social engagement. **Athens**, as the country's capital, offers a wide range of cultural, social, and nightlife experiences, while **Lesbos** holds historical significance within the queer community, with its connection to the poet Sappho, a prominent figure in the celebration of same-sex love.

---

25 https://www.globalcitizensolutions.com/lgbt-rights-in-greece/

However, while many areas of Greece are supportive and inclusive, there are still regions where acceptance may be more limited. **Thessaloniki**, a smaller city with a strong influence from the Greek Orthodox Church, is generally considered less tolerant of the LGBTQ+ community. Visitors in these areas may encounter more conservative attitudes, which contrast with the progressive atmosphere found in Greece's larger cities. Despite this, Greece remains a highly appealing and safe destination for LGBTQ+ travelers, offering a combination of culture, inclusivity, and scenic beauty that caters to the needs and desires of its diverse visitors.[26]

Public displays of affection (PDA) are generally accepted in Greece, but it is advisable for LGBTQ+ individuals and couples to exercise discretion in certain contexts. In more rural or conservative areas of the country, particularly those influenced by the Greek Orthodox Church, it is recommended to limit displays of affection in public spaces.

It is important for LGBTQ+ travelers to remain vigilant and aware of their surroundings, ensuring they are in safe and welcoming environments. Being conscious of local attitudes, especially when outside urban centers or in areas with less progressive views, can help minimize potential risks. It is always advisable to verify that the area being visited is LGBTQ-friendly, to ensure a safe and enjoyable experience.[27]

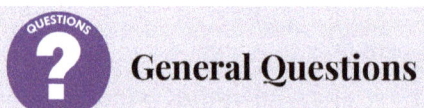 **General Questions**

1. ***Do laws in Greece protect homosexual expressions and conduct? Yes.*** Due to the legalization of same-sex marriage, there is nothing legally that restricts the expression of the LGBTQ+ community. That includes there being no laws against it.

---

26 https://www.thegreekvibe.com/
    lgbt-travel-in-greece-where-to-go-what-to-know/

27 https://greeking.me/blog/tips/gay-greece-travel

2. *What is the punishment for homosexual expressions and conduct?* There is no **punishment** for LGBTQ+ expression and conduct in Greece.

 **Law of the Land True Story**[28]

Stefanos Kasselakis, 35, made history as the first openly gay leader of Greece's SYRIZA party, a significant political shift for the leftist group now rebranded as the Progressive Alliance. Despite SYRIZA's current struggles with just 47 seats in the 300-member Greek Parliament, Kasselakis' surprise election victory over former labor minister Effi Achtsioglou garnered attention from both local and international media, including the American LGBTQ magazine Out. The magazine highlighted his potential to become Greece's first openly gay Prime Minister, noting that his background as a businessman—having worked for Goldman Sachs, attended the University of Pennsylvania's Wharton School, and run a shipping company—was in contrast to SYRIZA's traditionally anti-business stance.

Kasselakis' rise is stirring some controversy within his party, particularly from left-wing members who are uneasy with his capitalist background. Despite this, he has been vocal about pushing for progressive reforms, including advocating for the legalization of same-sex marriage in Greece. While Kasselakis has yet to outline a detailed political platform, his leadership marks a bold departure for SYRIZA as it looks to rebuild its influence ahead of the next elections in 2027.

---

28 https://www.thenationalherald.com/
lgbtq-magazine-sees-kasselakis-being-greeces-first-gay-premier/

 **Law of the Land Hypothetical**

HYPOTHETICAL: *I'm an LGBTQ+ tourist in Athens, and I see a group of religious people walking toward me. I'm openly gay, and I'm not sure how to handle this situation. What should I do to stay safe and respectful while being true to myself?*

ANSWER: *In this situation, the best approach is to remain calm and respectful. Greece is increasingly LGBTQ-friendly, particularly in urban areas like Athens, but you never know the specific views of people you might encounter. It's always a good idea to prioritize your safety and comfort while traveling. If you see a religious group approaching, consider keeping a respectful distance. You don't need to hide or change who you are, but out of courtesy (and to avoid any potential tension), it might be wise to allow them to pass by without engaging too much. Just as you would want your identity to be respected, it's also important to show respect to others.*

SEXUALLY MOTIVATED/ VIOLENT CRIMES

CHAPTER 9

SEXUALLY MOTIVATED/ VIOLENT CRIMES

Overview

Sexually motivated crimes, such as sexual assault, harassment, and trafficking, are present in Greece, as they are in many countries. However, the extent and prominence of these issues can vary depending on the specific type of crime and the context.

In Greece, certain groups are particularly vulnerable to sexually motivated crimes, and their experiences often reflect broader social and cultural challenges. Women, especially younger women, are the most affected by sexual assault and harassment. Many face these dangers in public spaces or within their own homes, yet the fear of social stigma and victim-blaming can make it hard for them to speak out, particularly in more conservative areas.

LGBTQ+ individuals, particularly transgender people, also face heightened risks. In larger cities like Athens, there is a more visible and accepting LGBTQ+ community, but in rural or more traditional regions, discrimination and harassment are still prevalent. Transgender sex workers, who often lack resources and protection, are especially vulnerable to exploitation and violence.

Migrants and refugees, particularly women and children, are also at great risk, especially within refugee camps or during their perilous journeys.

These individuals are often targets of sexual violence and human trafficking, finding themselves without the support they need to escape exploitation.

Sex workers, again particularly those who are migrants or transgender, are among the most at-risk groups, frequently facing sexual assault, exploitation, and abuse. Many are forced into precarious situations with limited options for help or escape.

Children and adolescents are another vulnerable group, with many falling victim to sexual abuse and exploitation, both within Greece and through trafficking networks. Online abuse is also on the rise, with the internet becoming a platform for sexual exploitation of minors.

Even tourists, particularly women and LGBTQ+ travelers, are not immune. In popular tourist areas, where alcohol and party culture dominate, they too may find themselves at risk of sexual harassment or assault, making it essential for travelers to stay vigilant.

Recent Statistics

Recent statistics reveal a troubling increase in sexually motivated violent crimes in Greece, especially against marginalized groups, including the LGBTQ+ community. In 2023, the Racist Violence Recording Network (RVRN) registered 158 attacks, a sharp rise from 74 in the previous year, with 61 targeting LGBTQ+ individuals. This increase is exacerbated by a culture of underreporting due to fear of discrimination and a lack of trust in law enforcement.[29]

The statistics indicate that many individuals experience both physical and sexual violence, with 39% of Greeks reporting a rise in violence toward the LGBTQ+ community. A significant portion, 91 percent, of those attacked did not report their incidents to the police. Factors contributing to this violence include socio-political dynamics influenced by

---

29 https://www.reuters.com/world/europe/
   racist-violence-surges-greece-report-finds-2024-04-23

conservative values and the Orthodox Church, which foster societal stigma and reluctance to report crimes.[30]

The implications for policy are significant, as the rise in sexually motivated violent crimes emphasizes the need for comprehensive legislative reforms and enhanced protective measures for victims. The government has begun implementing various initiatives, but practical support for marginalized groups remains inconsistent. Advocacy for stronger anti-discrimination laws and better resources for victims is essential in addressing the pervasive nature of sexual violence.

Related Legislation

Greece has made significant progress in addressing sexually motivated crimes through evolving legislation, driven by increasing social awareness and advocacy for sexual violence victims. Key developments include the 2019 amendment to the Penal Code, which redefined rape to focus on the absence of consent rather than physical resistance, aligning the law with international human rights standards. This shift is reflected in the updated Greek Criminal Code, where sexual assault is now defined with a clear emphasis on non-consensual acts.[31]

In response to growing societal concern and the MeToo movement, Greece has introduced further legislative measures, such as stricter penalties for sexual offenses and extended statute of limitations for crimes against minors. The legal framework has also expanded to include new forms of sexual violence, like online harassment and "revenge porn."

Recent amendments to hate crime legislation (2024) have strengthened protections against crimes motivated by sexual orientation and gender identity, addressing increasing hate crimes against LGBTQ+

---

30 https://fra.europa.eu/sites/default/files/fra_uploads/lgbtiq_survey-2024-country_sheet-greece.pdf

31 https://www.amnesty.org/en/latest/press-release/2019/06/greece-newly-amended-rape-law-is-a-historic-victory-for-women

individuals. These laws aim to create a safer environment for marginalized communities.

Despite these advancements, challenges remain in enforcing the laws. Victims often face societal stigma and reluctance to report crimes, with only 9 percent of sexual violence incidents being reported to the police. Advocacy groups continue to call for systemic reforms in the legal and judicial systems to ensure that all sexually motivated crimes are handled with the seriousness they require.[32]

 **General Questions**

1. *Do laws in Greece related to sex crimes protect the victims equally?* Greek laws about sex crimes aim to protect victims equally, with recent reforms strengthening protections, like focusing on consent in rape cases. However, societal attitudes, victim-blaming, and biases can hinder full protection, especially for women and marginalized groups. Despite legal progress, effective implementation and addressing cultural biases remain challenges.

2. *Pursuant to law, what is the age of consent for sex in Greece?* According to law, the age of consent in Greece is **18 years old**.

---

32 https://tribune.com.pk/story/2286245/
    greece-to-toughen-laws-on-sex-crimes-after-wave-of-abuse-allegations

Law of the Land Hypothetical

HYPOTHETICAL: *Maria, a tourist from Italy, is harassed by her tour guide in Athens, who makes inappropriate comments and touches her. She confronts him, and he apologizes, but she feels uncomfortable and decides to report it. Maria has a witness and photos of the guide. What should she do?*

ANSWER: *Maria should report the incident to the nearest police station in Athens, providing all evidence, including photos and a witness statement. She should keep the evidence secure and avoid sharing it publicly. To navigate the legal process, she should contact the Italian embassy for support and consider consulting a local lawyer to understand her rights. If needed, Maria should also seek counseling to process the emotional impact of the experience. These steps will help ensure her complaint is taken seriously and that she receives the necessary support.*

Takeaways

- Vulnerable groups, including women, LGBTQ+ individuals (especially transgender people), migrants, and sex workers, are at higher risk of sexually motivated crimes due to discrimination, stigma, and inadequate protection.

- Recent statistics show a troubling rise in sexually motivated violence, particularly against marginalized communities, with many cases unreported due to fear of discrimination and mistrust in law enforcement.

- Greece has made progress in addressing sexual violence through legislative reforms, but enforcement remains challenging due to societal attitudes, victim-blaming, and limited resources.

- Despite legal advancements, stronger anti-discrimination laws, and better victim support are needed, especially for marginalized groups facing pervasive sexual violence.

ARRESTED IN GREECE

CHAPTER 10
ARRESTED IN GREECE

Overview

When traveling in a foreign country, it is essential to recognize that you are subject to the legal jurisdiction and regulations of that nation. These laws may differ considerably from those in your home country and may not provide the same legal protection to which you are accustomed. It is important to understand that penalties for violating local laws may be far more severe than those for similar offenses in your home country, and ignorance of these laws is generally not accepted as a valid defense.

The consequences for violating laws while abroad can be significant and may include expulsion, fines, arrest, or even imprisonment. Even unintentional violations can result in serious legal repercussions. Therefore, travelers must make a concerted effort to familiarize themselves with and adhere to the laws of their host country to avoid potential legal entanglements, ensuring a safe and enjoyable experience during their travels.

Many countries impose strict penalties for offenses related to the possession, use, or trafficking of illegal drugs. Offenders who are convicted may face severe consequences, such as lengthy prison sentences and substantial fines. The legal process for foreigners arrested abroad typically involves being charged, prosecuted, and potentially convicted and sentenced, with the option of appealing the decision in certain cases.

Navigating a foreign legal system can be complicated, and individuals arrested abroad must be prepared to comply with the legal procedures of the host country. Seeking professional legal representation and gaining an understanding of the local legal landscape are crucial steps for those who find themselves facing legal challenges in a foreign jurisdiction.

Overall, awareness of and adherence to the laws of a foreign country are crucial components of responsible international travel. Understanding the potential consequences of legal violations and being prepared to navigate the legal system in the host country are essential in ensuring both safety and compliance during travel.

Arrest Process

Greece's criminal law addresses a broad range of offenses, each of which may result in severe penalties depending on the gravity of the crime. Among the most common criminal cases are theft, assault, and fraud, all of which can lead to significant legal consequences for the individuals involved.

The arrest process in Greece follows procedures that are aligned with international standards, outlined by the United Nations. Those arrested in Greece are typically required to remain in custody until their court hearing unless they can post bail. In some cases, individuals may be permitted to await trial outside of jail, but this is usually subject to certain conditions, such as restrictions on leaving the country. This can present challenges for foreigners who are arrested, as they may face additional complications related to travel restrictions and legal obligations during the waiting period.

Under Greek law, anyone arrested must be brought before a competent examining magistrate within 24 hours of their arrest. Foreign nationals in Greece go through a series of legal procedures, including preliminary examinations, questioning by a judge, and interactions with prosecutors. After these steps, the individual typically remains in custody unless granted bail. The time it takes to schedule a court hearing can vary significantly, with some cases taking several months, depending on the offense and the court's caseload. This delay can add considerable stress, especially for foreigners who are unfamiliar with the Greek legal system.[33]

Rights of the Arrested Person

Like many other countries within the United Nations and across Europe, Greece ensures that individuals who are arrested, including foreign nationals, have access to a range of fundamental rights. These rights are designed to protect individuals' dignity and ensure fair treatment during the detention process.

Firstly, detainees have the right to be informed in writing of the reasons for their detention. If the detainee does not understand the language used, they can request that the police provide a translation or explanation of the critical points of the decision in a language they understand. Additionally, detainees have the right to receive visits from family members and legal representatives, and they can have friends deliver necessary items such as clothes or money through the police.

Foreign detainees, like all those arrested, also have the right to consult with a lawyer and receive legal assistance. They are entitled to access telephone services and request medical care, including the provision of a doctor if needed. Detainees are given daily access to a designated outdoor area for exercise and fresh air, and they are provided with basic necessities, including a separate bed, clean sheets, personal hygiene items such as shampoo, toothpaste, and sanitary products.

For female detainees, the law mandates that they be held separately from male detainees, except when they are accompanied by family members and give consent to share the same space. Importantly, all detainees must be treated with dignity and respect, and any form of ill-treatment, including acts of racism, discrimination, or xenophobia, is strictly prohibited by law.

---

33 https://advocateabroad.com/greece/arrested-in-greece/

Furthermore, detainees have the right to report any concerns about their treatment, including potential ill-treatment or racial discrimination, to the Ombudsman. The Ombudsman is an independent authority tasked with investigating such complaints. Reports can be submitted directly by detainees at the Ombudsman's offices, ensuring that their rights are upheld, and any abuses are addressed appropriately.[34]

Getting Legal Assistance

The right to legal counsel for both defendants and suspects is firmly protected under both the Greek Constitution and the Code of Criminal Procedure. These legal frameworks ensure that individuals facing criminal charges are guaranteed access to qualified legal representation throughout the course of their proceedings. Moreover, the specific role of the defense lawyer is critically examined in relation to various procedural stages, including arrest and interrogation, highlighting the importance of their involvement in safeguarding the rights of the accused.

In the event of an arrest in Greece, it is crucial for anyone—regardless of nationality—to cooperate fully with the Hellenic Police and adhere to the procedures in place. Demonstrating respect and cooperation with law enforcement officers can lead to a more favorable and smoother experience throughout the process. Additionally, providing the police with all necessary identification is essential to avoid complications that may delay the legal proceedings. Doing so ensures that the case is handled efficiently, and the individual can move through the judicial process as swiftly as possible.

Embassies serve as official representations of a country in foreign lands, with a primary role of assisting their citizens abroad. If a foreigner is arrested in Greece, they have the right to contact their home country's embassy. The embassy can help contact family, friends, or employers of the detained U.S. citizen with their written consent, visit the detained U.S. citizen in jail, help ensure that prison officials provide appropriate

---

34 https://globalinvestigationsreview.com/insight/know-how/extradition/
report/greece

medical care, explain the local criminal justice and legal processes, and most importantly, connect you to local attorneys

American citizens may notify the U.S. Embassy or consulate of the arrest using the American Citizens Services Contact Form that can be accessed at **https://gr.usembassy.gov/** or directly at

U.S. Embassy in Athens

91 Vasilisis Sophias Ave
10160 Athens, Greece
Phone: +30-210-721-2951

Or

U.S. Consulate in Thessaloniki

Tsimiski 43, Thessaloniki 546 23, Greece
Phone: +30 231 024 2905

Bear in mind, however, that their powers are limited, and they cannot get U.S. citizens out of jail, provide legal advice, represent U.S. citizens in court, serve as official interpreters or translators, nor can they pay your legal, medical, or other fees.

Although there is a large number of attorneys, particularly in larger cities like Athens and Thessaloniki, who are fluent in English, the U.S. Embassy and consulates can also provide a list of English-speaking lawyers in Greece if needed. It's advisable to verify a lawyer's language skills, their experience working with international clients, and area of expertise before engaging their services.

Bail

As previously outlined, individuals who are arrested in Greece are eligible to apply for bail, which follows the procedures commonly observed in many other countries within the United Nations. This system allows individuals who have been detained to remain outside of jail while awaiting their court date, providing an opportunity to avoid prolonged incarceration before their trial. In order to access the option of bail, the defendant must submit a formal petition to the court, requesting a release order. Upon receiving the petition, the court has the discretion to either approve or reject the request based on factors such as the nature of the offense, flight risk, and any prior criminal record.

While the bail system is generally the same for both Greek nationals and foreign nationals, there are specific considerations for foreigners. One significant aspect is that foreign nationals, even if granted bail, may be required to stay in the country which can be challenging for foreign nationals, especially if the waiting period for their court hearing is extended. In some cases, the delay between the arrest and the trial can be several months, further complicating matters for foreigners who may have logistical or personal reasons for wanting to return home.

It is lesser known that Greek law allows a defendant to apply for a release order pending their court hearing. This provision details that a foreign detainee can petition for a more lenient arrangement, whereby they commit to regularly reporting to the Greek Embassy in their home country. This option can effectively enable the defendant to return home safely while ensuring they fulfill their court obligations when required. Nevertheless, specific conditions must be met, including proof of residence in their home country and established ties, like employment or family responsibilities.[35]

Complaints Against Police

Greece has one of the highest police-to-citizen ratios in the European Union, ranking second overall, yet it faces a significant and long-standing issue with police violence and misconduct. Historically, this issue has been particularly pronounced in instances of abuse directed toward minority groups and political dissidents. Furthermore, the country has been repeatedly criticized for violating human rights, which have become a common and troubling aspect of the Greek police force's operations.

---

35 https://advocateabroad.com/greece/arrested-in-greece/

Among the most frequent complaints lodged against law enforcement in Greece are allegations of false arrests. Many individuals report being unjustly detained, with little to no legal justification for their arrest. Additionally, there is widespread concern over the systemic discrimination faced by minority communities, including ethnic and racial minorities, as well as marginalized political groups. Another grave issue reported by the public is the excessive and inappropriate use of force by the police. In many cases, individuals who are arrested do not offer any resistance, yet they still face violent treatment during their detainment. These reports highlight significant concerns regarding the professionalism and conduct of the police, underscoring the urgent need for reforms aimed at ensuring greater accountability, improving police training, and protecting the rights of all individuals, regardless of their background or political stance.[36]

Filing a Complaint Against Police

To file a formal complaint against the police in Greece, an individual must first submit their grievance directly to the police station involved. If the issue is not resolved at the local level, the complainant has the right to escalate the matter to the Ombudsman, an independent government official responsible for investigating complaints related to public services, ensuring accountability and addressing concerns raised by the public.

When submitting a complaint to the Ombudsman, it must be in writing (not necessarily in Greek), include full identification and a signature, and be explicitly addressed to the Ombudsman with a request for intervention. Contact details such as a postal address and phone number are required for communication during the investigation. The complaint should outline the issue in detail, including the public service involved (e.g., the police), actions taken, outcomes, and any supporting evidence. Complaints can be submitted in person or by mail, providing an accessible way for individuals to seek redress and hold public services accountable.

---

36 https://ereb.eu/story/the-greek-justice-system-is-turning-a-blind-eye-to-police-violence-against-minorities/

When filing a complaint against the police in Greece, organizations like the **Hellenic League for Human Rights (HLHR)** and the **OHCHR Regional Office for Europe (ROE)** can provide crucial support. The HLHR, as Greece's oldest human rights organization, offers legal advice, advocacy, and guidance through the complaint process. They work to raise awareness of police abuse and can intervene in cases of human rights violations. **Victims can contact the HLHR via email (info[@] hlhr.gr) or phone (+30 2130264975) for assistance in ensuring their case is heard.**

The OHCHR ROE, representing the United Nations in Greece, can assist if local remedies, like filing a complaint with the Ombudsman, are ineffective. They offer technical support, advocacy, and international attention for serious cases of police brutality. **The OHCHR can be reached at (ohchr-InfoDesk@un.org) or phone (+41 22 917 9220) for those seeking further recourse.** [37]

? General Questions

1. *If I am convicted in Greece, am I likely to be released on bail pending the outcome of my appeal?* In Greece, whether you can be released on bail pending an appeal depends on the nature of the conviction and the court's assessment of flight risk or danger to public safety. Bail is more likely for less serious offenses, but for serious crimes, such as violent offenses, it is less common. Your lawyer would need to demonstrate that you are not a flight risk and will comply with conditions, such as reporting to the police. Ultimately, the judge makes the decision based on the specifics of your case. While bail is possible, it's not guaranteed, especially for serious convictions with long sentences.

---

37 https://www.gov.gr/en/org/astynomia/kataggelies

2. ***Who is entitled to bail?*** In Greece, most individuals convicted of non-serious crimes are entitled to bail, particularly if they have no prior criminal history and do not pose a flight risk or threat to public safety. However, those convicted of serious crimes, such as violent offenses or crimes with severe penalties, are less likely to be granted bail. Ultimately, the decision is at the discretion of the judge.

3. ***If I am arrested, how soon will I see a judge or magistrate?*** If you are arrested, you must be brought before a judge or magistrate within **24 hours** of your arrest. This is in line with Greek law, which requires that an arrested individual be informed of the charges and their rights and be given the opportunity to challenge the lawfulness of the arrest. If you are arrested outside of regular working hours, the court will usually arrange for an urgent hearing as soon as possible. If the judge or magistrate determines that there is no sufficient legal basis for your detention, they may order your release.

4. ***Will I be able to contact my country's embassy in Greece?*** Yes. If you are arrested in Greece, you have the right to contact your country's embassy. Greek law ensures foreign nationals can access consular assistance, which includes notifying your embassy, helping with legal support, and assisting with communication or informing your family.

5. ***If I am convicted, do I have to serve my entire sentence in Greece?*** A U.S. citizen incarcerated in Greece can apply to transfer their sentence back to the USA under the Council of Europe Convention on the Transfer of Sentenced Persons. The transfer requires mutual agreement from both the Greek and U.S. governments, with specific eligibility criteria, including being a U.S. citizen, having a punishable offense in both countries, and having a portion of the sentence remaining. The transfer process can take time and depends on both countries' approval.

CHAPTER 11

JAILS VS. PRISONS: CONDITIONS & CULTURE

IN THIS CHAPTER

- Overview
- Prison Conditions and Living Environment
- Inmate Rights and Legal Protections
- General Questions

JAILS VS. PRISONS: CONDITIONS & CULTURE

Overview

Jails and prisons are prevalent across the world, with conditions varying significantly from one country to another. The same disparity is evident within Greece, where the standards and functions of detention facilities can differ widely depending on the facility and the status of the individuals detained.

In Greece, jails are specifically designed to detain individuals who are suspected of committing a crime and are awaiting trial. These facilities serve as temporary holding centers for those who have not yet been convicted but are in the legal process, facing charges. On the other hand, prisons in Greece are intended for individuals who have been convicted of crimes and sentenced to serve time as part of their punishment. Prisons in this context are designed with a focus on both retribution and deterrence. Their purpose is to ensure that those found guilty of criminal offenses are detained and prevented from committing further crimes. These individuals are removed from society, and the experience of imprisonment is intended to deter them from reoffending once they are released, by providing an opportunity for reflection on their actions.[38]

---

38 https://www.raphaelrowefoundation.org/latest-news/
the-purpose-of-prisons

The Greek prison system faces significant challenges, particularly over-crowding, abusive management practices, and a lack of proper oversight. Overcrowding, with some prisons operating at over 149 percent capac-ity, leads to severe health and safety risks, exacerbating mental health issues, and fostering violence.[39] Abusive behavior by prison staff creates an atmosphere of fear, preventing inmates from reporting mistreatment. The lack of sufficient regulation and accountability allows these abuses to persist, as oversight mechanisms are weak. These issues not only af-fect inmates' well-being but also contribute to a failed rehabilitation sys-tem, increasing recidivism and undermining public trust in the justice system. The broader social impact is a cycle of crime and reoffending, re-inforcing prisons as punitive institutions rather than places of reform.[40]

Encouragingly, recent initiatives in Greek prisons focus on rehabilita-tion, offering educational programs to help inmates acquire skills for reintegration into society. The Greek Ministry of Justice, in collabora-tion with the European Council, is addressing issues like police brutality and torture, aiming to improve inmate treatment and uphold human rights. These efforts seek to create a supportive environment for person-al growth, encouraging inmates to engage in educational activities and motivating self-improvement, with the broader goal of enhancing the human rights landscape and overall well-being of prisoners.

Prison Conditions and Living Environment

Greek prisons follow a security classification system similar to those of other European nations, with levels ranging from Low to Administrative. **Low-security prisons** house inmates who do not pose significant threats and require minimal supervision, whereas **administrative-se-curity prisons** are designated for individuals who present higher risks and need more intensive monitoring and control. Inmates placed in the administrative category are often subjected to solitary confinement, a

---

39 https://lab.imedd.org/en/
overcrowding-isolation-and-shrinking-of-human-rights-in-greek-prisons

40 https://www.trtworld.com/life/greek-prison-conditions-overcrowd-ed-dangerous-poor-council-of-europe-60402

practice that has been criticized for its potential to cause severe psychological harm and cruelty.

A major issue in Greek prisons, as in many other countries, is **overcrowding**, which exacerbates the need for additional staff and resources. This strain often results in many facilities being classified as medium-security, where inmates experience reduced mobility and are under constant surveillance.

While prisoners in Greece are entitled to healthcare, access to medical services is often contingent on their behavior and their placement in cells where they are deemed trustworthy. Unfortunately, overcrowding, combined with the harsh conditions imposed by prison guards, frequently results in prisoners being denied medical care, even when it is urgently needed. This includes neglect of regular check-ups or treatment for injuries, especially those sustained due to interactions with prison staff. The **lack of adequate healthcare** and the **mistreatment of inmates** remain significant challenges within the prison system.

Greek prisons have long struggled to meet the basic needs of their populations, and the rising number of incarcerated individuals has only intensified these challenges. **Food rations** in many facilities are insufficient, failing to provide the necessary nutrition for prisoners. Overcrowding exacerbates these issues, leading to poor sanitation and inadequate living conditions. Inmates are often forced to endure these substandard conditions, contributing to the overall degradation of the prison environment.[41]

Inmate Rights and Legal Protections

In Greece, in theory, prisoners are entitled to challenge their arrest or imprisonment if they believe it was unlawful or lacked proper justification. This right ensures that individuals have a means to seek legal recourse when they feel they have been wrongfully detained.

---

41 https://www.prisonobservatory.org/upload/PrisonconditionsGreece.pdf

While prisoners are also entitled access to healthcare, mental health services, and basic necessities, the severe issues of overcrowding and the lack of regulation of prison personnel have effectively undermined these rights. In many cases, prisoners either face significant obstacles in obtaining the care and support they are entitled to, or they are unaware of the full scope of their legal rights due to inadequate information or lack of resources.

Greek prisoners retain the right to access legal assistance, including the ability to consult with lawyers and appeal court rulings if they believe their conviction was unjust or their arrest was unlawful. This provides an important avenue for prisoners to challenge legal decisions and seek a fairer judicial process.

While prisoners have these rights on paper, their practical implementation is often hindered by the challenges within the prison system. Such rights are often undermined in practice by overcrowding, lack of resources, and inadequate information. Overcrowded conditions limit access to necessary services, and prisoners may struggle to contact lawyers or fully understand their rights. Additionally, poor regulation and management abuse contribute to a system where rights are not always respected, making it difficult for inmates to effectively exercise legal protection.

 **General Questions**

1. *What is the difference between a jail and prison in Greece?* In Greece, **jails** are for those awaiting trial or serving short sentences, often for minor offenses, while **prisons** house individuals convicted of more serious crimes with longer sentences. Prisons generally have more structured facilities but both face overcrowding and poor conditions.

2. ***Do jails and prisons offer religious services to inmates?*** **Yes.**
   In Greece, religious services, primarily focused on Orthodox
   Christianity, are offered in many prisons. Led by priests, these
   services include prayer, sacraments, and counseling, providing
   inmates with spiritual support. Such practices are seen as key to
   rehabilitation, offering inmates purpose and community, which
   may help reduce recidivism.

3. ***How do prisoners spend their time?*** In Greek prisons,
   prisoners typically spend their time in a mix of mandatory and
   voluntary activities. Many are engaged in basic routines such
   as work assignments, which may include tasks like cleaning or
   prison maintenance. Educational programs, though limited, are
   available in some prisons, offering opportunities for inmates
   to earn qualifications or learn new skills. Recreational activities, such as exercise in outdoor yards, are also provided to help
   with physical well-being. However, overcrowding and a lack of
   resources often limit the availability and quality of these programs, leaving inmates with little constructive or meaningful
   engagement.

4. ***What type of jobs can inmates perform?*** In Greek prisons, inmates can perform a variety of jobs, including tasks like cleaning,
   maintenance, and kitchen work. Some prisons also offer voca-
   tional training, allowing inmates to work in areas such as car-
   pentry, tailoring, or agriculture. These jobs aim to help inmates
   develop skills and maintain prison operations, but opportunities
   are often limited due to overcrowding and a lack of resources.

5. ***How does the prison commissary system work in Greece?*** In
   Greece, the prison commissary system allows inmates to purchase basic goods such as food, hygiene products, and clothing
   using funds sent by their families or earned through prison work.
   The items available for purchase are limited and can vary depending on the prison's resources and budget. Inmates typically
   use a personal account to keep track of their funds, and the selec-
   tion in the commissary may be restricted due to overcrowding or
   financial constraints.

6. ***What type of medical care do prisoners receive?*** In Greece, prisoners are entitled to medical care, including general health-care, emergency treatment, and access to mental health services. Medical staff, including doctors and nurses, are present in most prisons, though the quality and availability of care can vary. Due to overcrowding and underfunding, there are often limitations in terms of resources, leading to delays in treatment or inadequate healthcare in some facilities. Inmates may also face difficulties accessing specialized care, and mental health services are often insufficient, despite the recognition of their importance in the rehabilitation process.

7. ***What is prison culture in Greece?*** Prison culture in Greece is shaped by overcrowding, limited resources, and strong inmate alliances based on shared backgrounds or regions. This creates a hierarchical structure with tension and occasional violence, both among inmates and between inmates and staff. While some prisons offer educational or religious programs to reduce tension, the overall culture is marked by a survival mentality due to harsh conditions and limited rehabilitation opportunities.

CHAPTER 12

HELPING A FRIEND OR RELATIVE IMPRISONED IN GREECE

IN THIS CHAPTER

- Overview
- Sending Food, Supplies, and Money to an Inmate
- Mail, Phone Calls, and Visitation
- Prison Scams
- Upon Release

CHAPTER 12

HELPING A FRIEND OR RELATIVE IMPRISONED IN GREECE

Overview

If you get arrested while traveling in Greece, it's important to stay calm and respectful toward the authorities. Comply with the police and avoid escalating the situation. You have the right to remain silent, so you can choose not to answer questions if you feel it's necessary. One of your first actions should be to request legal representation. In Greece, you are entitled to have a lawyer, and it's crucial to have one to help you navigate the legal process.

You should also ask to contact your embassy or consulate as soon as possible. They can provide vital assistance, such as helping you understand the legal system, ensuring your rights are upheld, and offering support in finding legal representation. Additionally, you have the right to notify your family or a close friend about your arrest, so they can help with resources like financial support or contacting a lawyer on your behalf.

Make sure to ask for a clear explanation of the charges or the reason for your arrest, as you are entitled to know why you're being detained. It's also essential to cooperate with the legal process, attend any necessary hearings, and explore options for appealing or defending yourself with your lawyer's guidance. By staying informed and utilizing the resources available, you can ensure that your rights are respected and navigate the situation as smoothly as possible.

Furthermore, as Greece is a member of the United Nations, if there are concerns regarding the sufficiency of assistance provided by the U.S. Embassy in Greece, family members or friends have the right to seek support from any other U.S. Embassy located in a European Union member state that is part of the UN. This ensures that there are multiple avenues for obtaining assistance and ensures that the individual's rights are upheld within the framework of international law.[42]

Hiring an English-speaking attorney in Greece is crucial for non-Greek speakers, especially if you are facing legal issues such as arrest or charges. The legal process can be complex, and understanding the local laws, procedures, and your rights is essential to ensuring a fair trial or outcome. An English-speaking lawyer can help bridge any language barriers, ensuring you fully understand the charges, your legal options, and the steps involved. They can also communicate effectively with the authorities and courts on your behalf, preventing misunderstandings that could negatively affect your case.

Additionally, an English-speaking attorney can assist in navigating the Greek legal system, which may differ significantly from your home country's legal processes. This includes helping you understand the nuances of Greek law, handling official documents, and providing advice tailored to your situation. Without proper legal assistance in your language, you risk making critical errors that could impact your defense or cause unnecessary delays.

 A list of English-speaking attorneys can be accessed at **https://advocateabroad.com/greece/lawyers/**.

Sending Food, Supplies, and Money to an Inmate

In Greece, while food rations are often limited and stretched thin, prisoners still have access to basic sustenance. However, the quality of the meals they receive is typically poor, with common offerings including

---

42 https://travel.state.gov/content/travel/en/international-travel/emergencies/arrest-detention.html

low-quality gyros and simple dishes such as spaghetti. When available, prisoners may receive limited servings of vegetables and fruits.

Greek prisoners are entitled to receive two or three meals a day, depending on the resources available within the prison system. The frequency and quality of meals can vary based on the availability of supplies and the discretion of the prison staff. Additionally, the allocation of food can be influenced by the conduct of the prisoners, as those deemed to have misbehaved or violated rules may find themselves further restricted.

The types of supplies you can send to inmates are carefully regulated for both security and hygiene reasons. Generally, acceptable items include basic clothing, such as underwear, socks, and casual wear, although it's important to follow the prison's guidelines, which might restrict items like clothes with logos or inappropriate symbols. Personal hygiene items, like soap, toothpaste, shampoo, and deodorant, are also allowed. Reading materials, including books and magazines, are typically permitted, especially educational or religious texts. Inmates can also receive stationery for writing letters, as well as prescribed medication, provided it comes with proper documentation from a doctor.

However, there are several items that are strictly prohibited. Perishable foods, like fresh meat, fruits, or dairy products, are not allowed, as they pose health and safety risks. Alcohol and drugs are, of course, forbidden, and any sharp objects, such as knives or scissors, are also banned. Electronic devices, including mobile phones and radios, cannot be sent in, as they may be used for unauthorized communication. To avoid confusion or delays, it's always best to check directly with the specific prison for their most current guidelines on what can and cannot be sent to an inmate, ensuring that the items comply with all regulations.

Additionally, cash is not allowed to be sent directly to an inmate; instead, money must be deposited into the prisoner's account through official channels. Families and friends can send money to inmates through various methods, primarily using remittance services. Some commonly utilized services include Western Union, MoneyGram, and Xoom.[43]

---

43 https://www.revolut.com/en-US/money-transfer/send-money-to-greece/

Each service offers its unique features, such as different fees and transfer speeds, but all provide a reliable means to get money into the hands of inmates. When choosing a remittance service, it is essential to compare rates and ensure that the selected service operates within the specific prison system where the inmate is located.

To initiate a transfer, the sender typically needs to provide the recipient's full name, the prisoner's identification number, and any additional information required by the service. Additionally, it is advisable to inquire directly with the remittance service regarding processing times and any specific instructions pertinent to sending funds to Greek prisons.

Mail, Phone Calls, and Visitation

Mail

The process of sending mail to inmates in Greek prisons is generally straightforward, but it's also governed by strict rules. Friends and family can send letters to incarcerated individuals, and the good news is that **mail is not read or censored**, which allows for open communication between the inmate and their correspondents. Each prison facility may have its own requirements; therefore, it is advisable to verify these details with the specific prison's administration to prevent any setbacks in the delivery of mail.

Phone Calls

Inmates in Greek prisons are not allowed personal cell phones. Instead, they can receive incoming calls from family or friends, but these too are heavily regulated. Calls are monitored and recorded for security reasons, and all conversations are overseen by prison guards. Inmates are typically allowed a set amount of phone time per month, usually around 500 minutes, which means calls must be kept brief.

If an inmate is found with an illegal cell phone, it can lead to severe consequences, including additional prison time, hefty fines, or loss of privileges. Prison staff may also conduct thorough searches to track down the source of the unauthorized phone. These stringent rules are aimed at maintaining order and preventing illicit activities within the prison, though they can complicate communication for prisoners and their families.

Visitation

Generally, inmates have the right to receive visits, but the frequency and nature of these visits can fluctuate based on the inmate's status. Convicted prisoners are entitled to at least one visit per week, whereas individuals awaiting trial may receive visits twice a week.[44]

Family members seeking to visit inmates must carry formal proof of their relationship, such as birth or marriage certificates. This policy is essential for ensuring that only authorized individuals are permitted to communicate with inmates. For friends and family who do not share the same last name as the inmate, permission must also be obtained from the prison authorities beforehand. This requirement serves to uphold security and manage visitation effectively.

Different types of visitations can occur in Greek prisons, including face-to-face visits and those conducted in specially designated areas that accommodate families, particularly when children are involved. Additionally, a new correctional code in Greece has allowed conjugal visits in certain circumstances, reflecting efforts to improve inmate welfare.

In instances where an inmate's circumstances permit, they may also receive visits from consular staff as an additional support mechanism. However, security measures, such as a thorough search of all visitors and their belongings, are in place to prevent the introduction of contraband.

It is important to note that the **duration of visits is typically limited to 30 minutes** unless a special request is made and approved by the prison authorities. Additionally, visits are monitored by prison staff to ensure

---

44 https://www.gov.uk/government/publications/greece-prisoner-pack/
    information-pack-for-british-prisoners-in-greece

compliance with all regulations, which dictates a controlled environment during such interactions.

Prison Scams

While Greece remains generally considered a safe country to live in, its prison system, as discussed throughout this section, has notable challenges. While it is unlikely that a prisoner will directly fall victim to a scam, the friends and family of convicted felons are far more likely to encounter fraudulent schemes.

One of the most prevalent scams to be cautious of involves individuals who claim they can assist with organizing **bail for the prisoner**. These scammers typically contact individuals by phone, presenting themselves as reliable figures who can facilitate the transfer of bail funds. In reality, they exploit the situation by convincing people to send money to them, only to disappear with the funds.

It is important to remember that the U.S. Embassy often provides assistance in handling bail arrangements, and such arrangements should only involve official representatives, not unknown individuals reaching out by phone. Additionally, bail payments are always made directly to the prison authorities and should never be sent to a third party.

Another common scam is **legal assistance fraud**, when scammers pose as "legal consultants" or attorneys and claim that they can secure a reduced sentence, an early release, or special treatment for the inmate in exchange for a substantial fee. They may ask for payment upfront, promising to provide legal services or initiate appeals, even though they have no legal knowledge or intention to help.

Also be aware of **prisoner phone fraud**, whereby a scammer may pretend to be an inmate calling from prison. These calls are often made collect or require the recipient to add funds to an inmate phone account. Once the scammer establishes contact, they may claim to be the inmate, asking for money to cover a variety of expenses (such as bail, legal fees, or emergencies). Sometimes, they may even impersonate the voice of the actual inmate to convince the family member that it's a legitimate call.

If there is any suspicion of a scam, it is crucial to cease all communication with the scammer and avoid sharing any personal or sensitive information. Furthermore, the suspicious contact should be reported to the local authorities, who can investigate the issue. In cases where funds have already been transferred, it is strongly recommended to immediately notify the bank to cancel any cards or accounts associated with the transactions.[45]

Upon Release

When a foreign national is released from prison in Greece, there are no unique or special regulations governing their departure beyond standard protocols. The only requirement is that the individual must be accompanied by an escort who will ensure their safe return to their home country. This escort may be a family member, legal representative, or a designated individual arranged through the appropriate authorities, such as the U.S. Embassy.

Aside from this stipulation, there are no additional legal obligations or restrictions placed on foreign nationals upon their release. Once a foreigner has completed their sentence and is allowed to return to their home country, they are not permanently barred from reentering Greece. Therefore, it remains possible for the individual to visit Greece again in the future, provided they comply with the applicable visa and entry requirements at that time.[46]

---

45 https://www.forbes.com/sites/walterpavlo/2023/08/25/bureau-of-prisons-warns-of-scams/

46 https://advocateabroad.com/greece/arrested-in-greece/

THE ADMINISTRATION OF JUSTICE

THE ADMINISTRATION OF JUSTICE

Greece's Legal System

Greece's legal system has undergone significant transformations throughout its history. In the early stages, prisons and jails as we know them today were virtually nonexistent. Instead, individuals who were awaiting punishment were kept in holding cells. These early forms of detention primarily housed those awaiting execution for their crimes. Execution was one of the few forms of punishment, alongside exile and public humiliation, which were considered common practices for punishing offenders. These punitive measures, however, were viewed more as deterrents than actual solutions, designed to instill fear of severe consequences such as exile or death, even for relatively minor offenses like petty theft. The introduction of human rights principles and a shift toward more ethical treatment ultimately brought an end to such practices, leading to the development of a more humane legal system with a broader range of options for punishment and reform.

The evolution of the Greek legal system is tied to the establishment of the democratic government, although the formation of structured legal systems and the creation of organized police forces were not immediately part of this transition. For many years, the country lacked a unified police system, and local cities often had their own legal frameworks, with few written laws or official records of criminal activity. In these cities, appointed magistrates typically oversaw trials and determined sentences, often without the structured judicial processes seen today.

The modern Greek legal system is grounded in key principles that reflect the country's history. These core components include written law, codification, and the separation of powers. The practice of maintaining written laws is central to the Greek system, ensuring transparency and accountability for both the legal professionals and the individuals involved in legal proceedings. Codification further organizes these laws into coherent structures. One of the most important elements of the system is the separation of powers, which divides governmental authority into three branches: the legislative, executive, and judicial branches. This structure is designed to prevent the concentration of power in any single branch or individual, ensuring a system of checks and balances.

Similar to the United States, Greece's legal framework is built around a system of courts, which is organized into three distinct branches. The legislative branch is represented by the Greek Parliament, responsible for lawmaking. The executive branch consists of the Greek Cabinet, comprising the government and heads of various ministries. The judicial branch, which oversees the interpretation and application of laws, includes the Supreme Judicial Court and the Special Supreme Tribunal.

Legal procedures in Greece vary in duration depending on the complexity of the case. Typically, the process begins with the formal opening of the courtroom, where the judge, lawyers, and the accused are introduced. The charges are presented, and witnesses are heard, followed by a mandatory mediation session that provides all parties with time to reflect on the case. Afterward, evidence and arguments are presented in full, culminating in a hearing where the case is reviewed comprehensively by the judge and jury. The proceedings conclude with the issuance of the verdict and sentence, which may include fines, imprisonment, or other forms of judgment. Following the verdict, there is an opportunity for an appeal, marking the official close of the case as the defendant begins to serve the sentence.[47]

---

47 https://generisonline.
    com/a-comprehensive-overview-of-the-legal-system-in-greece/

The Judiciary

The judiciary represents the established system of courts within Greece, tasked with overseeing the legal proceedings for individuals accused of committing crimes, ranging from minor infractions such as traffic violations to more serious offenses. It plays a critical role as the foundation of the nation's democratic principles, reflecting the deep and longstanding connection between democracy and the judicial system in Greece. The judiciary ensures the fair and impartial administration of justice, making it an essential component of the country's governance and rule of law.

At the grassroots level, there are **local courts** known as *Eirinodikeia*, which form the foundational tier of the Greek judicial structure. These courts handle a wide spectrum of civil and criminal matters, including minor disputes, misdemeanors, and violations of regulatory laws, ensuring that even smaller issues are addressed efficiently. The role of *Eirinodikeia* courts is pivotal, as they serve as the entry point for many legal matters before they advance to higher levels of jurisdiction.

Beyond these local courts, Greece's judicial system is organized into several **specialized court** divisions: civil justice, penal justice, and administrative justice. **Civil justice courts** are responsible for overseeing cases involving individuals who have been arrested, categorizing offenses from the least severe to the most serious. The judgments rendered in these courts determine the fate of the accused, setting the tone for subsequent legal actions. **Penal justice courts** handle more serious criminal cases, particularly felonies, and often employ a "mixed" court system, wherein professional jurors, who are experienced in legal matters, work alongside ordinary citizens serving as jurors. Lastly, **administrative justice courts** address conflicts between citizens and public authorities, handling matters that involve governmental and institutional issues.

Distinct features of Greece's judiciary include the bifurcated jurisdictions of administrative and civil courts, each addressing different forms of disputes. The "mixed" court system, wherein both professional and lay jurors work together, further enhances the flexibility of the system. Professional jurors, who are employed as part of the judicial process, provide their expertise over multiple cases, which allows for more consistent and informed decision-making.

However, the judicial system faces several challenges, the most notable being the requirement for all cases to undergo an initial review by the civil justice courts. This process often results in substantial delays, as the time between filing a case and securing a court date can take up to 18 months. As a result, individuals accused of crimes may spend over a year in jail while awaiting their trial, which places significant strain on both the accused and the overall judicial system. This backlog in the legal process highlights the need for reforms to streamline the system and reduce unnecessary delays.[48]

 **General Questions**

1. *Will the court treat first-time offenders and tourists with more leniency?* In Greece, first-time offenders and tourists may receive some leniency, particularly for minor offenses like traffic violations or petty theft. First-time offenders might benefit from alternative sentences such as fines or community service, while tourists may have the option to settle cases with fines. However, leniency depends on the severity of the crime and the circumstances, with more serious offenses leading to stricter penalties regardless of the offender's status.

2. *If I am charged with a crime, which court is likely to hear my case?* In Greece, the court that hears your case depends on the crime's severity. Local courts (*Eirinodikeia*) handle minor offenses, while penal courts deal with serious crimes like felonies. For some severe cases, mixed courts with both professional and lay jurors may be involved. If the case involves disputes with government authorities, it would be heard in administrative courts. The specific court is determined by the nature of the charge.

---

48 https://generisonline.com/understanding-the-hierarchy-and-roles-within-the-judicial-system-of-greece/

3. *What is the standard of proof in a criminal case in Greece?*
   In Greece, the standard of proof in a criminal case is "beyond a reasonable doubt." This means that the prosecution must prove the defendant's guilt to such an extent that no reasonable doubt remains in the mind of the judge or jury. The burden of proof lies with the prosecution, and the defendant is presumed innocent until proven guilty. If the prosecution fails to meet this high standard, the defendant must be acquitted.

Law of the Land True Story [49]

The term *Heliaia* or *Heliaea* in ancient Greece referred to the supreme court of Athens, which played a crucial role in the development of Athenian democracy and legal systems. Comprised of over 6,000 male citizens selected by lot, the court was responsible for enforcing laws and administering justice in a rapidly evolving democratic society. Located in Athens, the Heliaia handled a wide range of cases, from public offenses to more serious crimes, ensuring that legal proceedings reflected the democratic principles of equality and collective responsibility.

By incorporating citizens directly into the judicial process, the Heliaia marked a significant shift from monarchic or aristocratic rule, laying the foundation for modern democratic and legal practices. Its decisions were instrumental in shaping Athenian law and establishing precedents that influenced future legal systems.

---

49 https://www.britannica.com/topic/Greek-law

Takeaways

- Greece's legal system evolved from ancient practices of execution, exile, and humiliation, shifting toward a more humane and structured system influenced by democratic principles and human rights.

- The system includes local courts (*Eirinodikeia*) for minor offenses, penal courts for serious crimes, and administrative courts for disputes involving government authorities. Some serious cases are heard in mixed courts, combining professional and lay jurors.

- In criminal cases, the standard of proof is "beyond a reasonable doubt," with the prosecution bearing the burden of proof. Defendants are presumed innocent until proven guilty.

- While the system ensures justice, there are challenges, such as delays in case processing, with some cases taking up to 18 months for a court date, which leads to significant strain on the judicial process.

CHAPTER 14

CRIME VICTIM ASSISTANCE

CHAPTER 14

CRIME VICTIM ASSISTANCE

Overview

Under Greek law, individuals who fall victim to a crime within the country are granted comprehensive support services free of charge. This assistance is available before, during, and after the occurrence of the crime, ensuring that victims receive the help they need at every stage of their experience. The support provided is specifically tailored to address the unique circumstances of each victim, recognizing that every case is different and requires a personalized approach.

In Greece, crime victims have access to a range of resources aimed at providing support throughout the legal process and aiding their recovery. The Greek Ministry of Justice offers victim support services, including legal assistance, psychological counseling, and guidance through the criminal justice system. Victims can reach out to helplines like **SOS Helpline** (**15900**), which offers immediate assistance for domestic violence victims, and the **National Hotline for Victims of Crime** (**116006**), which provides information about legal rights and available resources.

For those unable to afford legal representation, legal aid is available, and victims can seek assistance from advocacy groups like **KETHI**, which provide both legal and psychological support, especially to victims of gender-based violence or trafficking. Psychological counseling centers across the country offer therapeutic services to help victims of various crimes cope with trauma.

Victims of domestic violence have access to shelters and safe houses, where they can find temporary housing, counseling, and legal aid. Additionally, the **Victim Compensation Fund** provides financial assistance to those affected by violent crimes, helping cover medical expenses and other costs. Foreign nationals may also be eligible for compensation through the European Union's compensation scheme.

Victims can report crimes at local police stations, where specialized units handle sensitive cases such as domestic violence and trafficking. The court system also offers support, providing accommodations during legal proceedings and allowing victims to testify via video if necessary to protect their privacy.

Non-governmental organizations (NGOs), such as the **Greek Council for Refugees (GCR)** and other social services, provide further assistance, especially for victims of trafficking or sexual violence, ensuring that they receive the help they need to recover. Migrants and refugees, in particular, can access networks tailored to their specific needs, including language support and specialized legal aid. These resources work together to ensure that victims in Greece receive comprehensive support in their recovery journey and during their interaction with the justice system.

Emergency Preparedness

While traveling in Greece, it is advisable to connect your mobile phone to local network towers to ensure access to the country's emergency numbers. Additionally, it is recommended to familiarize yourself with and have easy access to these emergency contacts to effectively manage any potential emergencies while abroad. Consider saving some of these numbers into your phone contacts before you travel to Greece:

- **Emergency:** 112
- **Ambulance:** 166
- **Fire Department:** 199
- **Police:** 100
- **Coast Guard:** 108

- **Hospitals:** 106
- **General Telephone Assistance:** 11888

What to Do if You Are the Victim of a Crime

If you become a victim of a crime in Greece, your priority should be to ensure your safety. If you're in immediate danger, call emergency services at **112** or **100** for the police. Once safe, report the crime at the nearest police station, providing as much detail as possible. If you've been physically harmed, seek medical attention immediately, as injuries should be documented by healthcare professionals for potential legal proceedings.

After ensuring your safety and health, you can access various victim support services available in Greece, discussed in the section above depending on the nature of the crime. Victims can also explore legal aid options if they cannot afford representation, ensuring they understand their rights and receive proper assistance through the legal process.

In addition to immediate support, victims may be eligible for **compensation** through Greece's Victim Compensation Fund, which can help cover medical costs and lost income due to the crime. Foreign nationals may also apply for compensation through the EU Victim Compensation Scheme. It's important to stay informed about your case by following up with the authorities and exploring additional resources.

One of the most crucial steps in any kind of crime is that the foreign national promptly reports the incident to their embassy, which can provide them with vital resources and guidance at such a trying time. Seeking professional help is strongly recommended, particularly in cases involving legal proceedings. Holding the perpetrator accountable is an essential part of the recovery process for any victim, and providing the necessary information to aid in locating or prosecuting the offender is vital.

Common Tourist Scams in Greece

While Greece is renowned for its hospitality, it is not immune to scams that target unsuspecting tourists. Probably the most widespread is pickpocketing that can occur in both crowded and less crowded areas, with criminals often taking advantage of unsuspecting tourists. It is strongly advised to always keep a close eye on valuable items, as children, in particular, may exploit their ability to maneuver through crowds to target victims.

Another common issue in Greece involves counterfeit goods sold by street vendors who may charge exorbitant prices for items that are worthless or poorly made. Tourists may be misled into purchasing goods that are not worth the price paid, or in some cases, completely useless. In addition, there are widespread scams related to photographs and tickets for tourist attractions. Scammers may offer photos of monuments or tickets to historical sites, but in many cases, the photos are of poor quality or non-existent, and the tickets are either invalid or counterfeit, often leaving tourists with nothing of value.

To avoid falling victim to such scams, tourists should always keep their valuables secure and within sight, ideally storing them in bags tightly secured to their bodies. Wallets, keys, and other personal items can be safeguarded by attaching them to chains or securing them to clothing. It is also crucial to remain cautious of individuals who appear overly friendly or persistent, as this behavior can be indicative of an attempt to scam. Tourists should avoid purchasing goods from unreliable vendors and should refrain from buying tickets for attractions from anyone who cannot provide verifiable proof of affiliation with the site.

It is highly recommended for tourists to stay alert, conduct thorough research on the areas they plan to visit, and be mindful of their surroundings. Taking these precautions can help prevent the distress and inconvenience caused by stolen belongings or financial loss, ensuring a more enjoyable and secure travel experience.

Sexual Assault

In the unfortunate event that a foreigner becomes a victim of sexual assault in Greece, it is essential to remember that the assault is never the victim's fault. Sexual assault is a grave violation, and every victim has the right to seek help and take steps to bring their abuser to justice. For foreigners who experience such an incident in Greece, it is strongly advised to report the assault to their home country's embassy and the local police as soon as possible to streamline the process. Reporting the assault is a critical step in seeking justice.

Once the victim has reported the incident, understanding their legal rights and accessing the necessary support services are crucial. This includes immediate medical care—both physical and psychological—which is essential for the victim's recovery. Medical treatment should be prioritized as it can help assess and treat injuries, as well as provide crucial evidence for legal proceedings.

Victims of sexual assault in Greece have the right to both medical and government assistance. If the perpetrator poses an ongoing threat to the victim, the government can provide protection and security measures. Furthermore, the victim has the right to pursue legal action against the perpetrator in court, using their own medical records and other evidence to support their case. Greece's legal framework ensures that victims have access to free support services, including counseling, medical care, and legal aid, in accordance with their rights as victims of crime.[50]

 **Safety Recommendations**

▪ Avoid traveling alone for extended periods, especially in less populated or higher-risk areas.

---

50 https://www.gov.uk/government/publications/greece-information-for-victims-of-rape-and-sexual-assault/greece-information-for-victims-of-rape-and-sexual-assault

- Never accept invitations from strangers or individuals you do not know well.

- Keep emergency numbers readily accessible and easily reachable.

- Stay in areas with a visible police presence or large groups of people.

- Trust your instincts; if something feels uncomfortable or unsafe, leave the area immediately.

- Research your destination beforehand to familiarize yourself with safe zones and areas to avoid.

Consular Assistance

Consular assistance is an essential resource for citizens who find themselves victims of a crime while in Greece. When a foreign national experiences a crime, they may face significant challenges, especially if they are unfamiliar with the local legal system, language, or cultural context. In these situations, consular support becomes crucial. Consular officials can provide vital legal guidance, helping the victim understand their rights under Greek law and offering explanations of the legal process. This is particularly important since legal proceedings can be complex, and having the support of someone who understands both local laws and the victim's rights is invaluable.

Language barriers often add to the stress of dealing with a crime abroad, and consular staff can bridge this gap by offering translation and interpretation services. This ensures that the victim can effectively communicate with the police, healthcare providers, and legal professionals, without fear of misunderstanding. Beyond this, consular officials can connect the victim with local support services, such as legal aid, victim support organizations, or emergency shelters, ensuring they receive the care and assistance they need to recover.

Additionally, consular officials play a critical role in advocating for the victim's safety and well-being. They can assist in securing protection, help manage interactions with local authorities, and offer support if the victim feels unsafe or vulnerable. In cases where the victim may wish to return to their home country, consular assistance can facilitate repatriation, offering a sense of security in what may be an emotionally and physically overwhelming time. Ultimately, consular assistance serves as a lifeline, providing both practical help and emotional support during an incredibly difficult experience.[51]

While embassies play a crucial role in assisting citizens who become victims of crime abroad, there are limits to what they can do. They cannot provide legal representation, cover legal costs, or intervene in local judicial processes. They also cannot offer monetary compensation, provide physical protection, or handle personal matters like canceling credit cards. While embassies can offer advice, connect victims with local resources, and help with travel arrangements, their role is primarily to guide and support rather than directly resolve legal or financial issues.

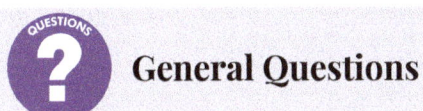 **General Questions**

1. *If I am a victim of a crime, can I legally be compensated?* **Yes.** If you are a victim of a crime in Greece, you may be eligible for compensation, particularly if the crime is violent, such as assault or rape. Greece has a victim compensation fund to help cover medical expenses, funeral costs, and lost earnings. To qualify, the crime must be reported to the police, and the victim must meet certain conditions. Additionally, victims can seek compensation from the perpetrator through the courts. It's recommended to consult legal professionals for guidance on eligibility and options.

---

51   https://embassynvisa.com/
     embassy-services-for-expats-what-you-should-know-living-abroad/

2. *If a family member falls victim to homicide, can I bring the body back to my home country?* **Yes.** You can bring a family member's body back to your home country if they fall victim to homicide in Greece. The process involves obtaining a death certificate and clearance from Greek authorities, which may depend on the ongoing investigation. You can then work with a funeral home or repatriation service to handle transportation. It's also advisable to contact your embassy for assistance with necessary documentation.

3. *If a family member falls victim to homicide, will I receive any assistance from the Greek government?* **Yes.** If a family member falls victim to homicide in Greece, you may receive assistance from the Greek government. This can include support through the victim compensation fund, which helps cover funeral costs, medical expenses, and other related expenses. The authorities will also provide guidance on legal matters, such as reporting the death and navigating the judicial process. Additionally, the Greek government may assist with repatriation procedures for the body, though you may need to work with your embassy for further support.

CHAPTER 15

POLICE

IN THIS CHAPTER

- Overview
- Police Response
- Police and Community Relations
- Police Use of Force
- Law of the Land True Story

POLICE

Overview

The Greek Police Force, known formally as the **Hellenic Police**, is charged with a broad array of responsibilities, including maintaining public order, enforcing laws, and ensuring the safety of citizens. Despite its critical role in society, the force faces several significant challenges, including issues concerning staffing adequacy, public trust, and allegations of excessive force.

The Hellenic Police is comprised of various operational units distributed across the country. While specific figures can fluctuate, estimates place the total number of personnel in the police force at around 50,000. This includes officers responsible for general policing duties, traffic enforcement, and specialized units that tackle organized crime and terrorism. In recent years, the structure of the Greek police has evolved, seeking to address emerging security challenges and improve law enforcement efficacy in response to crisis situations, particularly amid rising crime rates and increased immigration pressures.[52]

Based on reports, there is a general consensus that the force is under-staffed due to an increasing demand for police services and limited recruitment efforts. An alarming statistic indicates that only one police officer is available for every 1,300 citizens, which raises concerns about the

---

52 https://www.astynomia.gr/hellenic-police/?lang=en

ability of the force to effectively manage security and respond to emergencies.[53] Moreover, there have been calls for a comprehensive review of staffing levels across various branches to enhance operational capacity. In critical areas such as asylum processing and crime prevention, there remains a pronounced need for more officers, highlighting the inadequacy of current staffing figures.

The Greek Police Force faces several pressing issues impacting its functionality and reputation. One of the most significant concerns is the growing public distrust and dissatisfaction regarding police conduct. Reports of excessive use of force and police brutality have surfaced repeatedly, feeding a narrative of institutional failings within the Hellenic Police. For instance, a recent European Court of Human Rights ruling highlighted cases of violence and inadequate investigation procedures, which have contributed to a culture of fear among minority communities.[54]

Moreover, allegations of corruption and collusion with organized crime have come to the fore, undermining the credibility of the police force. Instances where officers were arrested for complicity with drug trafficking emphasize the need for an internal overhaul to ensure accountability and restore public confidence.[55]

Additionally, systemic issues such as inadequate training, high levels of occupational stress, and insufficient mental health resources for officers exacerbate the challenges faced by the Greek Police Force. The force grapples with a pressure-cooker environment, where the expectations to maintain order clash with the reality of limited resources and mounting public discontent.

---

53 https://eur-lex.europa.eu/legal-content/EN/TXT/
    HTML/?uri=CELEX:32016H0193

54 https://www.errc.org/press-releases/european-court-rules-against-greek-
    police-who-beat--tortured-roma-in-2016

55 https://www.reuters.com/world/greek-police-officer-arrested-suspi-
    cion-helping-major-drug-ring-2024-11-29

Police Response

The Hellenic Police, like law enforcement agencies worldwide, holds a broad range of responsibilities aimed at maintaining public order and safety. These duties include ensuring peace and order, performing general policing tasks, and overseeing traffic safety. Additionally, the police are charged with preventing and suppressing crime, safeguarding the state, and implementing national security policies.

As Greece's national police force, the Hellenic Police primarily handles domestic civil matters and law enforcement within the country. In contrast, the Hellenic Armed Forces, the Greek military, is tasked with addressing larger-scale national defense and security issues. Furthermore, the Hellenic Coast Guard plays a critical role, particularly given Greece's geographical position as an archipelago. The Coast Guard is essential for managing maritime issues, which are more prevalent in Greece than in landlocked countries.

The Hellenic Police are directly responsible for managing civil unrest within the country. Their duties include ensuring public peace, preventing and suppressing criminal activity, and consistently enforcing the law. Additionally, the police are tasked with preventing illegal entry or exit from Greece, overseeing border control for both tourists and migrants to maintain national security and compliance with immigration policies.[56]

The Hellenic Police Force is undergoing significant reforms aimed at improving accountability, integrating advanced technologies, and adapting to modern policing standards. These changes, which include a shift toward more restrained use of force and the adoption of technologies like AI and facial recognition, are challenging for officers who must adjust both their tactics and skills. Many officers are struggling with the new protocols and technology systems, requiring extensive training and support to ensure ethical and effective use. Additionally, the ongoing overhaul of the police and prison systems, supported by both the Greek government and the European Council, aims to restore integrity and ensure that law enforcement operates within national and international

---

56 https://www.wikiwand.com/en/articles/Greek_Police

legal standards. However, resistance to change, logistical difficulties, and concerns over privacy and accountability remain significant obstacles.[57]

Police and Community Relations

At present, the public image of the Hellenic Police in Greece is largely negative. A significant portion of the Greek population expresses fear and distrust toward their law enforcement officers, concerned about the potential of excessive use of force. Many citizens view the police as violent and overly aggressive, often perceiving them as focused on enforcing their duties in the quickest, and at times most extreme, manner possible. There are reports of harassment and humiliation directed at individuals suspected of committing crimes, which further fuels these negative perceptions.

This growing dissatisfaction has led some to believe that external intervention, particularly from the European Council, is necessary to address these concerns. Many citizens feel that the police have often evaded accountability for their actions, with some attributing this to perceived weaknesses within the Greek justice system. While it is unclear whether this is entirely accurate, the widespread belief in the system's inability to hold law enforcement accountable has contributed to a deep mistrust of both the police and the broader judicial framework. This sentiment highlights the urgent need for comprehensive reform to restore public confidence in Greece's law enforcement institutions.[58]

Police Use of Force

Police use of force is a significant issue in Greece, with concerns over excessive violence, especially during protests and in dealings with minority groups such as Roma and migrants. High-profile incidents of

57 https://www.ekathimerini.com/news/1247185/
measures-afoot-to-radically-transform-police-force/

58 https://murrowgoesgreek.weebly.com/our-stories/
public-perceptions-of-police-and-crime-in-greece

police brutality have led to public distrust and legal challenges, including rulings from the European Court of Human Rights condemning police actions. There are allegations of racial profiling, abuse, and inadequate investigations, contributing to a tense relationship between the police and marginalized communities. The Greek police are undergoing reforms to address these issues, with calls for greater accountability, transparency, and training in human rights and de-escalation techniques to ensure that force is used appropriately. However, changing institutional practices and restoring public confidence remain ongoing challenges.

 **Law of the Land True Story**

On April 1, 2024, 28-year-old Kyriaki Griva was murdered outside a police station in Athens by her ex-partner, marking the fifth femicide in Greece that year. Despite previous complaints against him, Griva chose not to report him again due to fear and lack of trust in the system. She requested a police escort, but was told patrol cars were "not a taxi service." The killing has sparked outrage, with calls for investigation into the officers' actions and for femicide to be legally recognized in Greece. Women's rights groups argue that domestic violence is not taken seriously by authorities, and many families of victims are demanding tougher penalties and systemic changes to protect women.[59]

---

59 https://www.aljazeera.com/features/2024/5/10/
    how-often-will-this-keep-happening-greece-reckons-with-rising-femicides

HOW TO GET LEGAL HELP IN GREECE

HOW TO GET LEGAL HELP IN GREECE

Available Resources

If you find yourself in legal trouble as a visitor in Greece, there are several resources available to help you navigate the legal system. Greece provides access to legal aid services for foreigners, including assistance with legal representation and advice. The **Athens Bar Association** (+30 210 3398102-3; info@dsa.gr) offers resources to help you find a local lawyer, especially for criminal cases. You can also contact your **embassy or consulate** for immediate legal support and guidance.

In addition, **the Ministry of Justice** provides information on free legal aid for those who cannot afford private legal services. Various organizations across Greece, such as **Diotima (https://diotima.org.gr)**, offer legal support for gender-based violence and other social issues, and they can provide guidance if you're facing legal trouble.

Another important resource is the **Tourist Legal Aid Network**, which helps people in need of legal services; you can access more information at **https://tourist.legal/tourist-legal-aid-greece/**. They offer assistance for a wide range of legal matters, from criminal allegations to civil disputes. Some local municipalities and community centers also provide free legal consultations or can direct you to the appropriate legal resources.

For those living outside major cities, **local police stations** can sometimes offer basic legal information or direct you to legal aid services available in your area. If you need to speak with a lawyer immediately, contacting your **embassy** should be a priority, as they can recommend trusted lawyers and help with communication.

In urgent situations, the **emergency number in Greece is 112**, which connects you to police, medical, or fire services, and can also assist in situations requiring immediate legal attention.

Legal Aid

Foreign visitors in Greece facing legal issues may be eligible for legal aid under specific conditions, depending on their financial situation. Greek law ensures that individuals, regardless of nationality, have access to legal assistance if they are unable to afford the costs of legal representation. This reflects the country's commitment to providing equal access to justice for all.

To qualify for legal aid in Greece, applicants must demonstrate insufficient financial resources to cover the costs of legal services. The assessment takes into account the individual's income and assets, and depending on their financial situation, they may be granted full or partial legal aid. This assistance applies to a wide range of legal matters, including criminal cases, civil disputes, and administrative issues.

Victims of domestic violence and certain crime victims may be entitled to legal aid without a financial assessment, reflecting Greece's focus on supporting vulnerable individuals.

To apply for legal aid, visitors must complete an application form, providing necessary documentation such as proof of identity, residency, and financial status. Once submitted, the legal aid office will review the application to determine eligibility based on the individual's financial condition and the nature of their legal issue. For further assistance, applicants can contact the local Bar Association or the Ministry of Justice.

Foreign Embassies in Greece

When foreign visitors find themselves in legal trouble while traveling or residing in Greece, their home embassy or consulate plays a crucial role in providing essential support and guidance. Embassies and consulates are responsible for ensuring that their citizens have access to the necessary resources during difficult legal situations, offering vital assistance to navigate the local legal system.

One of the primary functions of an embassy or consulate in legal matters is to provide critical information about the Greek legal system, including an overview of the judicial process and the rights of detained individuals. This guidance is especially important, as legal systems and procedures can vary significantly from country to country.

Embassies also help by connecting individuals with local resources, such as governmental and non-governmental organizations (NGOs) that may offer further legal support. They maintain lists of local attorneys who are fluent in the detainee's language and familiar with the Greek legal system, ensuring access to appropriate legal representation.

Here are some of the foreign embassies in Greece that can assist in legal matters:

U.S. Embassy
91 Vasilisis Sofias Avenue
Athens 10160, Greece
Tel: (+30) 210-721-2951
Website: gr.usembassy.gov

Canadian Embassy
1 Ploutarchou Street
Kolonaki, Athens 10675, Greece
Tel: (+30) 210-727-3700
Website: www.canadainternational.gc.ca/greece

British Embassy

1, Syntagma Square
Athens 10557, Greece
Tel: (+30) 210-727-2600
Website: www.gov.uk/government/world/organisations/
british-embassy-athens

Australian Embassy

1 Vassilissis Sofias Avenue
Athens 10674, Greece
Tel: (+30) 210-727-3300
Website: greece.embassy.gov.au

 For a full list of foreign embassies and consulates in Greece, visit **www.greeka.com/greece-travel/embassies**. These diplomatic missions are available to help citizens who face legal challenges while in Greece, ensuring they receive appropriate support and assistance during difficult times.

MEDICAL FACILITIES & HOSPITALS

IN THIS CHAPTER

- Overview
- Visitors' Access to Healthcare in Greece
- Greek Hospitals
- Medical Emergencies
- Insurance Guidance

MEDICAL FACILITIES & HOSPITALS

Overview

Greece has a healthcare system that combines both public and private sectors, aiming to provide universal coverage to all residents, including legal migrants. The backbone of the system is the **National Health System** (**ESY**), which is funded mainly through taxes and social insurance contributions. **Public healthcare** in Greece is generally accessible and offers comprehensive services, including hospital care, primary healthcare, and preventive treatments. The system is highly regarded for its strong emphasis on family medicine and preventive care, particularly in urban centers like Athens and Thessaloniki, where the healthcare infrastructure is better developed.

The public system, however, faces significant challenges, particularly in the wake of the 2011 economic crisis, which led to budget cuts, austerity measures, and increased strain on resources. The financial constraints have affected the quality and accessibility of services, with long waiting times for certain treatments and limited availability of medical staff in some areas. While the public system is still largely free or low-cost for residents, patients often face co-payments for medications and specialist consultations, which can be a financial burden for lower-income families. The rise of **private healthcare** in Greece, driven by a desire for faster access to services and higher comfort, reflects the growing demand for quicker, more personalized treatment. Private health insurance has become more common, especially among those who can afford it.

Although the public healthcare system offers universal access, accessibility remains a significant issue, particularly in rural areas. Urban centers generally have better access to modern medical facilities and specialists, whereas rural populations may experience delays in receiving treatment or must travel long distances to access necessary care. This disparity between urban and rural healthcare resources is one of the system's most pressing challenges.

Quality of care is generally high in the public sector, especially in urban hospitals where modern medical equipment and skilled professionals are available. However, in rural and remote areas, the quality of care can be more variable due to a lack of specialized services, outdated facilities, and fewer healthcare professionals. This uneven distribution of healthcare resources means that the quality of service often depends on where a patient lives, which can affect overall health outcomes.

Affordability is a persistent concern in Greece's healthcare system. While healthcare services are largely funded through taxes and social insurance, many people still face out-of-pocket costs for medications, specialist consultations, and other medical services. For example, co-payments for prescription drugs can reach up to 25 percent, which can be a significant burden for those with limited financial resources.[60] Despite the public healthcare framework providing relatively low-cost services, the economic reality for many families is that healthcare is not entirely free. This financial strain has led many Greeks to seek private health insurance, which offers quicker access to healthcare but at a higher cost.

Visitors' Access to Healthcare in Greece

Access to healthcare for visitors in Greece is generally good, though it varies depending on whether the visitor has health insurance, and the nature of the care needed.

Greece provides a well-established healthcare system for its residents, but visitors—such as tourists, business travelers, and short-term

---

60 https://immigrantinvest.com/blog/greece-healthcare-system-en/

residents—are not automatically covered by the ESY. Instead, they must rely on private health insurance or pay out-of-pocket for services. That said, Greece's healthcare services are of high quality, particularly in urban areas, and emergency care is available to all, regardless of insurance status.

For **emergency medical services**, visitors can receive treatment at public hospitals and healthcare facilities. **Emergency care in Greece is generally free of charge for tourists**, though non-emergency services typically come with a cost. The **112 emergency number** connects to ambulance services, and hospitals are well-equipped to handle urgent medical situations, including trauma, heart attacks, and other emergencies.

If a visitor needs **routine care** or treatment that is not considered an emergency, they will need to pay for services. This includes visits to general practitioners, specialists, or prescription medications. **Private healthcare providers** in Greece are commonly used by tourists who seek faster service or specialized care. In these cases, visitors can expect to pay higher fees, particularly for services such as consultations, diagnostic tests, or treatments.

Travelers should have **health insurance** to ensure that they are covered for any medical needs while in Greece. Most visitors are advised to obtain **travel insurance** that includes medical coverage before their trip. Many travel insurance policies also cover medical evacuation, which can be crucial in the event of a serious illness or injury in remote areas. Some countries, like those in the EU, may have a **European Health Insurance Card (EHIC)** that allows visitors from member states to access healthcare services at the same cost as local citizens, though it typically does not cover everything, such as private care or repatriation.

For those visiting Greece on long-term stays or for business or study purposes, it's highly recommended to have private health insurance, as the public healthcare system may not cover all costs for non-residents. In general, private hospitals and clinics offer a higher standard of care in terms of amenities and faster service, though they can be expensive without insurance.

Greek Hospitals

As of recent statistics, Greece boasts approximately 283 hospitals, which include both public and private institutions.[61] The public healthcare system, ESY, provides a large segment of these facilities, comprising around 130 general and specialized hospitals that serve the majority of the population.[62] In addition to hospitals, Greece has around 280 private healthcare facilities operating in conjunction with public resources, providing over 45,900 beds across the country.[63] However, despite the availability of facilities, there are notable concerns regarding the distribution of resources, quality of care, and access to services in remote areas.

The concentration of hospitals in Greece is primarily urban, with most hospitals located in densely populated areas such as Athens and Thessaloniki. Approximately 55 percent of the hospitals in Greece are publicly owned, and these public hospitals account for two-thirds of all available hospital beds.[64] Urban centers benefit from a larger number of advanced medical facilities equipped with specialized care options and state-of-the-art technology compared to rural areas, where healthcare services may be limited.

The islands, especially those in the Aegean, typically have a lower concentration of healthcare facilities. While there are an adequate number of hospitals on islands such as Crete and Rhodes, smaller islands may struggle with fewer healthcare options, resulting in longer travel times for residents needing medical care. The variability in healthcare access is pronounced in remote regions and isolated islands, creating disparities in healthcare availability and access.[65]

---

61 https://www.internationalinsurance.com/hospitals/greece

62 https://www.trade.gov/country-commercial-guides/greece-healthcare

63 https://www2.deloitte.com/content/dam/Deloitte/gr/Documents/life-sciences-health-care/gr_healthcare_in_greece_noexp.pdf

64 https://freopp.org/greece-25-in-the-2024-world-index-of-healthcare-innovation/

65 https://www.researchgate.net/publication/364756688_Regional_Distribution_Disparities_of_Healthcare_Resources_in_Greece

In addition to hospitals, Greece has a network of primary healthcare centers spread throughout the country. These centers provide general healthcare services, preventive care, immunizations, and outpatient services. Many of these are located in more populated areas, though some rural regions still struggle with adequate access.

Medical Facilities Catering to International Travelers

In Greece, international travelers have access to a range of medical facilities tailored to their needs, particularly in major cities like Athens and Thessaloniki, as well as in popular tourist destinations. Notable private hospitals such as **Hygeia Hospital** and **Athens Medical Center** in Athens, as well as **Interbalkan Medical Center** in Thessaloniki, offer high-quality care and are accustomed to treating foreign visitors. These hospitals provide both emergency services and specialized medical treatments, with multilingual staff and the ability to directly bill international insurance providers.

Additionally, there are travel clinics, like the **Athens Medical Center Travel Clinic**, which offer services like vaccinations, health consultations, and care for travel-related illnesses, ensuring that visitors can receive preventative care and treatment during their stay.

In tourist-heavy regions such as Crete, Rhodes, and Mykonos, smaller private clinics and health centers are also available to provide medical services for international visitors. These clinics, while not as large as urban hospitals, offer essential care and often cooperate with international health insurance companies for easier payment processes. Emergency medical services are widely accessible, and hospitals in major tourist areas are well-equipped to handle urgent medical situations.

Greece has also become a growing hub for **medical tourism**, with hospitals like **Mitera Hospital** and **Aretaeio Hospital** offering specialized treatments in fields like cosmetic surgery, dental care, and fertility, providing tailored services to meet the needs of foreign patients seeking high-quality medical care at competitive prices.

 **Medical Emergencies**

1. **What should you do if you feel unwell/sick in Greece?** If you feel unwell in Greece, start by assessing your symptoms. For mild issues like a cold or digestive discomfort, visiting a local pharmacy is a good option, as they can provide over-the-counter remedies and helpful advice. If your symptoms are more serious, seek care at a private clinic or hospital, many of which have English-speaking staff. In case of an emergency, dial 112 to request an ambulance, which will take you to the nearest hospital. If you have travel insurance, contact your insurance company for guidance on medical facilities and coverage options. For travel-related illnesses, visiting a travel health clinic, such as the Athens Medical Center Travel Clinic, may be particularly useful. Otherwise, if your symptoms are mild, ensure you rest and stay hydrated.

2. **What if you need hospital care in Greece?** If you need hospital care in Greece, your options depend on whether it's an emergency or not. For emergencies, call 112 for an ambulance, which will transport you to a public hospital. Emergency care in public hospitals is free for all visitors. For non-emergency care, you can visit a private hospital like Hygeia Hospital in Athens or Interbalkan Medical Center in Thessaloniki, which provide high-quality care and may have direct billing arrangements with international health insurers. It's advisable to contact your insurance provider before seeking care to ensure coverage and ease payment processes. In rural or island areas, local health centers or smaller regional hospitals may offer more basic services but may lack the specialized care available in larger cities.

Insurance Guidance

Many hospitals and medical facilities in Greece accept **foreign insurance plans**, particularly private hospitals and clinics that cater to international patients. These hospitals often have direct billing agreements with international insurance companies, which means they can directly process your claims, making the payment process easier for foreign visitors.

However, it's always a good idea to **contact your insurance provider** before seeking treatment to confirm that your plan will be accepted at the facility and to understand the claims process. Some insurance plans may require upfront payment, after which you can file for reimbursement. For this reason, it's essential to keep all receipts and medical documentation to submit to your insurance provider.

In public hospitals, foreign insurance may also be accepted, but the billing process can vary, and you may need to pay out-of-pocket and then seek reimbursement from your insurance company. If you have **travel insurance** or **international health insurance**, it's highly recommended to check the specific terms of your policy regarding healthcare coverage abroad.

 **Average Cost of Common Medical Services**

Healthcare in Greece is relatively affordable, particularly in public healthcare settings.

- For mild illnesses, visiting a **pharmacy** generally costs between €20-€40 (about US$22-$44) for non-residents, while private clinics charge between €40-€70 (about US$44-$77) for general consultations.

- **Specialist consultations** in the private sector range from €70 to €150 (about US$77-$165), and **emergency room** visits at private hospitals can cost anywhere from €100 to €300 (about

US$110-$330). Public hospitals provide free emergency care for residents, but foreign visitors may pay around €50-€150 (about US$55-$165).

- **Medical tests** like blood work or X-rays at public hospitals can cost €10-€50 (about US$11-$55) for visitors, while private facilities charge €30-€150 (about US$33-$165) depending on the test.

- **Hospital stays** in public hospitals are free for residents, with foreign visitors paying €50-€150 (about US$55-$165) per day. In private hospitals, daily rates range from €150 to €300 (about US$165-$330), and surgeries range from €1,000 to €5,000 (about US$1,100-$5,500).

- **Dental visits** typically cost €30-€60 (about US$33-$66) for a check-up, and medications range from €5 to €100 (about US$5.50-$110) depending on the prescription. Having travel insurance can help manage these costs, especially for major treatments and private care.

Foreign visitors to Greece typically pay for healthcare services either out-of-pocket or through their travel health insurance, depending on the situation. For most public and private facilities, visitors are required to pay upfront for services, especially if they are not covered by insurance.

If visitors have travel health insurance, many private hospitals, like Hygeia Hospital and Athens Medical Center, offer direct billing with international insurance providers, meaning the visitor may not need to pay upfront. In cases where direct billing is unavailable, visitors pay out-of-pocket and can later submit receipts for reimbursement through their insurance. Payments are typically made via credit card, debit card, or cash, and it's always advisable to check both with the healthcare provider and insurance company to understand the coverage and payment process before seeking treatment.[66]

---

66 https://immigrantinvest.com/blog/greece-insurance-en/

DRIVING IN GREECE

CHAPTER 18
DRIVING IN GREECE

Overview

Overall, Greece's **road infrastructure** is generally well-developed in urban areas and major tourist destinations. In cities like Athens and Thessaloniki, and along the main highways like the Egnatia Odos (which spans the north of the country) and the Attiki Odos (the Athens ring road), roads are typically in good condition. These roads are well-maintained, clearly marked, and modern, providing smooth driving experiences. The highways also have frequent service areas, rest stops, and signs in English, making them more accessible for foreign drivers. The National Road System, connecting major cities, also offers relatively efficient and safe routes for long-distance driving.

However, as you venture into rural areas, especially on smaller islands or mountainous regions, the condition of roads can vary significantly. In some places, roads might be narrow, winding, or even unpaved, with few or no road markings. The terrain can be challenging, especially on islands like Santorini or Crete, where roads might be steep and winding, requiring more cautious driving. Some rural roads can be rough, with occasional potholes or sharp turns, so it's important to drive slowly and carefully.

The traffic in Greece can also be a bit chaotic, especially in cities. Drivers tend to be less strict about following lane discipline, and there is frequent use of horn signals. Parking can be challenging in congested city centers, and in some areas, it's common to park in places that may seem unconventional, such as on sidewalks or near pedestrian crossings. Still, in tourist-heavy locations, like Athens or the islands, it is advised to be cautious and attentive to avoid fines.

In terms of **signage**, Greece provides good road signs, often with both Greek and English labels, making navigation easier for international visitors. However, in rural areas, signage might not be as frequent or as clear, so it's helpful to use a GPS or a map.

Speed Limits and Safety Regulations

Speed limits in Greece vary depending on the location. In urban areas, the speed limit is generally set at **50 km/h** (**30 mph**), while on open roads, the limit increases to 110 km/h (70 mph). It is important to remain vigilant and aware of posted speed limits and other signage, as they may differ between regions.

Greece adheres to many of the safety regulations common in the European Union, with strict standards in place to ensure driver and pedestrian safety. These regulations include a zero-tolerance policy for drinking and driving, the importance of staying alert and aware of your surroundings, ensuring regular maintenance of your vehicle, and respecting posted signs and speed limits. It is crucial to follow basic road laws to ensure a safe driving experience, especially considering the sometimes unpredictable road conditions and aggressive driving behavior.

Documentation and Insurance Requirements for Foreign Travelers

When driving in Greece, it's essential to carry a few key documents and ensure you have the right insurance coverage. If you're from an EU or EEA country, your valid EU driving license is sufficient, but if you're from outside the EU, you'll need an International Driving Permit (IDP) along with your national driver's license, especially if your license isn't in English or uses a non-Latin alphabet. Along with your license, you should always have your **passport** or **national ID card** on hand for identification, as you may be asked for it during a traffic stop.

If you're driving a rental car, you'll be provided with the **vehicle registration documents** by the rental company, and it's important to keep them with you. If you're driving your own car, make sure you have the **vehicle registration papers**. Additionally, you must carry **proof of insurance**. Third-party liability insurance is mandatory in Greece, so whether you're renting or using your own vehicle, ensure the policy is valid and covers you for driving in the country.

In terms of insurance, third-party liability coverage is required by law, but if you're renting a car, it's usually included in your rental agreement. For added peace of mind, you might also want to take out **Collision Damage Waiver** (**CDW**) insurance, which protects you in case of damage to the rental car. Theft protection is also an option, safeguarding against loss of the vehicle. **Personal Accident Insurance** (**PAI**) is another add-on you might consider for medical coverage in case of an accident.

If you're driving a car you own and are coming from outside the EU, it's recommended to bring a **Green Card**, an international insurance certificate.[67]

Toll Roads

You'll also need to be prepared for tolls on some of Greece's highways. Greece, with its combination of mainland and numerous islands, relies heavily on its road network for transportation across the country. Toll roads play a significant role in connecting various regions and facilitating travel between major cities and destinations. Greece is home to a network of nine toll highways, each designed to provide access to specific parts of the country.

When using these toll roads, drivers are required to make payments at designated toll booths. Payment is accepted exclusively in cash, with Euros being the only form of currency accepted. It is important to note that other methods of payment, such as credit cards or electronic payments, are not supported at these toll booths. As such, travelers should

67 https://www.tripsavvy.com/driving-rules-in-greece-1524185

ensure they have sufficient cash on hand to cover toll fees when using Greece's extensive highway system.[68]

Main Traffic Rules

Driving in Greece requires awareness of several key traffic rules and regulations, some of which may differ slightly from what drivers are used to in other countries. Here's an overview of the main traffic rules to keep in mind when driving in Greece.[69]

- **Speed Limits:** Speed limits in Greece are clearly marked, and it's important to adhere to them. On **highways**, the general speed limit is **130 km/h (81 mph)**, while on **rural roads**, it's usually **90 km/h (56 mph)**. In urban areas, the speed limit is typically **50 km/h (31 mph)**, though in residential areas and near schools, it may drop to **30 km/h (19 mph)**. Always watch for speed limit signs, as they can vary.

- **Seat Belts:** Seat belts are **mandatory** for all passengers, both in the front and rear seats. Failure to wear a seat belt can result in fines.

- **Alcohol Limit:** The legal blood alcohol limit in Greece is **0.5 g/L** for private car drivers, which is slightly lower than some other European countries. However, it's advisable to avoid drinking altogether if you're planning to drive. For professional drivers, the limit is even stricter at **0.2 g/L**.

- **Mobile Phones:** Using a mobile phone while driving is prohibited unless you are using a **hands-free system**. Police are strict about enforcing this law, and fines can be issued if you're caught using a phone without a hands-free device.

---

68 https://www.tolls.eu/greece

69 https://www.sixt.co.uk/magazine/tips/driving-tips-in-greece/

- **Parking:** Parking can be a challenge in busy urban areas like Athens. Be sure to park in designated areas. Parking in prohibited zones, such as near pedestrian crossings, on sidewalks, or in front of fire hydrants, can lead to fines or even towing. **Paid parking** zones are common in major cities, and it's important to pay attention to parking signs.

- **Roundabouts and Intersections:** At roundabouts, vehicles already inside the roundabout have the right of way. When driving through an intersection without traffic lights, vehicles coming from the right have the right of way. Always yield to traffic coming from the right unless indicated otherwise by road signs.

- **Headlights: Daytime running lights (DRLs)** are required on certain roads, particularly on highways, during daylight hours. In some rural or mountain areas, especially in foggy conditions or tunnels, it's also important to use headlights even during the day.

- **Indicators and Lane Discipline:** Using your **turn signals** (**indicators**) is mandatory when changing lanes or turning. Greek drivers are known for their aggressive driving habits, but it's essential to follow lane discipline and respect the flow of traffic.

- **Motorcycles and Scooters:** In Greece, motorcycles and scooters are common on the roads. Always be cautious, as they may move between lanes, especially in heavy traffic. Be sure to check your mirrors before changing lanes.

- **Child Safety:** Children under **10 years old** must be seated in the back seat, and children under **135 cm** (4'5") must use an appropriate **child safety seat** or booster.

- **Driving in Rural and Mountain Areas:** In rural or mountainous areas, roads can be narrow and winding. Always drive cautiously, especially on sharp turns or when visibility is poor.

- **Road Signs:** Greek road signs are generally clear, but some may be in Greek. It's advisable to familiarize yourself with the most common traffic signs before driving, though English is widely understood, especially in tourist areas.

General Questions

1. *Can I use my driver's license from my home country to drive in Greece?* **Yes.** You can use your driver's license from your home country to drive in Greece if you're a tourist. If you're from an EU/EEA country, your license is fully valid. If you're from a non-EU country, you'll need an International Driving Permit (IDP) in addition to your national driver's license, especially if it's not in English or uses a non-Latin alphabet. The IDP translates your license into multiple languages, including Greek, and ensures you comply with local regulations.

2. *What is the age requirement for renting a car in Greece?* In Greece, the minimum age to rent a car is typically **21**, though drivers under 25 may face an additional young driver surcharge. Most rental companies require drivers to have held a valid license for at least 1 year. Drivers over 70 may face age-related restrictions or higher fees. Always check the rental company's specific policies.

Law of the Land Hypothetical

HYPOTHETICAL: *Sarah, a 28-year-old tourist from the United States, decides to rent a car to explore the Greek islands. She picks up a car in Athens, and after a few days of sightseeing, she drives to the island of Santorini. The narrow roads on the island are winding, and visibility is limited due to fog. While driving cautiously around a sharp turn, Sarah hits a pothole that causes the car to lose control briefly, and she ends up grazing the side of a parked car. What should Sarah do after the accident? Is she liable for the damage to the other car, and how does her rental car insurance coverage work in this case?*

ANSWER: *After grazing a parked car in Santorini, Sarah should stop and contact the police, as is legally required in Greece. She should* *document the damage with photos and report the accident to create an official record for insurance. Her rental insurance, including Collision Damage Waiver (CDW), will likely cover the damage, but she should check her agreement for any deductible. If the parked car's owner is unreachable, she should leave her contact details. By following these steps, Sarah can handle the situation properly and ensure her insurance covers the costs.*

NUDE BEACHES & CLOTHING-OPTIONAL RESORTS

CHAPTER 19

NUDE BEACHES &
CLOTHING-OPTIONAL RESORTS

Overview

Nudist culture is not officially permitted in Greece, which may come as a surprise to many, especially given the country's rich historical legacy. Ancient Greece, known for its remarkable contributions to art, philosophy, and religion, often incorporated nudity into its cultural expressions. The practice was particularly evident in the reverence of the god Dionysus, who was associated with freedom, vitality, and physical expression. Nudity, especially in the context of religious rituals and athletic competitions, was a symbol of both purity and connection with nature.

However, despite this historical background, modern Greece does not officially embrace nudist culture. While there are no explicit laws prohibiting nudity, it is important to note that being nude outside designated areas is considered a serious breach of local decorum. Public nudity is generally seen as offensive to many locals, potentially leading to significant social disapproval. In certain cases, individuals may face fines or even arrest if caught engaging in nudity outside the designated spaces.

Though nudity is not openly embraced in most public settings, Greece does provide some opportunities for those wishing to experience naturism. Several nude or naturist beaches are legally accessible to the public, providing a safe and welcoming space for individuals to engage in nudism. Among the most popular are **Paradise Beach**, located on the western coast of Corfu Island. This beach, accessible only by boat, is known for its secluded, serene environment, making it a favored spot for those seeking a quiet retreat.

Another well-known destination is **Seitan Limania Beach**, located on a peninsula near Chania on the island of Crete. This stunning beach is framed by towering cliffs and offers a secluded atmosphere for visitors to unwind. **Agios Sostis**, located on Mykonos Island, is another popular naturist beach. The picturesque location, combined with the freedom it offers, attracts both locals and tourists alike who wish to experience a liberating beach environment.

Beyond public beaches, there are several hotels and resorts that cater specifically to the needs of naturists and nudists. Among the most recognized options are Saladi Beach Hotel and Vritomartis Cretan Naturalist Resort. **Saladi Beach Hotel**, conveniently located in Athens, is uniquely positioned with direct access to its own nudist beach, giving guests the opportunity to enjoy the freedom of naturism while remaining in proximity to the cultural and historical attractions of the Greek capital. The hotel also offers a variety of recreational activities, ensuring guests have a fulfilling and diverse stay.

On the island of Crete, **Vritomartis Cretan Naturalist Resort** stands as one of the most popular and well-regarded naturist resorts in Greece. This resort provides a comprehensive range of activities designed to cater to the interests of naturists, from boat rides along the coast to access to several other nude beaches. Guests can also enjoy a wide range of amenities, including scuba diving, massages, and wellness treatments. With its emphasis on relaxation and connection with nature, Vritomartis offers a truly idyllic experience for those looking to embrace a naturist lifestyle.[70]

Legality and Safety

Nudism in Greece is regulated through access to designated nudist resorts and beaches, where individuals are expected to respect both the

---

70 https://www.greeka.com/greece-holiday/naturism-nudism/

local norms and the comfort of others around them. It's important to note that while these areas offer a safe environment for naturists, visitors are expected to adhere to the rules of the space, including the requirement to put on clothing when leaving these designated zones. Failing to do so can result in significant consequences, including fines or even arrest. Therefore, it is crucial to remember that no level of personal expression justifies violating these rules and facing legal repercussions.

Nudists, especially tourists, should always be aware of their surroundings and the social and cultural norms of the places they visit. Understanding when and where nudity is appropriate is key. For instance, if a visitor arrives at a nudist beach and notices others are not nude, it's important to respect their choice. There could be local or cultural reasons for this, and visitors should adjust accordingly. Public nudity outside of designated areas is strongly discouraged, particularly in places not officially approved for nudism, as it can be seen as disruptive and disrespectful to the local community.

Moreover, particular care should be taken when in the presence of children. It is inappropriate and potentially uncomfortable for children to be in nudist or clothing-optional spaces. Visitors should refrain from bringing children to these areas, both to protect the children's well-being and to respect the boundaries of other guests who are seeking a comfortable and private environment. By following these guidelines, nudists can help ensure that their activities remain respectful and harmonious with the cultural norms and expectations of Greece.[71]

Safety should always be a priority, and you should consider the following factors:

1. **Research the Destination:** Look for established nudist beaches or resorts with good reviews. Online forums and social media can provide insights from fellow travelers about safety and experiences.

2. **Local Regulations:** Familiarize yourself with the rules of the specific beach or resort. Some places may have designated areas for nudism,

---

71   https://nomadicated.com/nudity-in-greece/

while others might be more lenient. Adhering to local customs helps ensure a positive experience.

3. **Travel in Groups:** If possible, visit with friends or fellow travelers. There's safety in numbers, and it can enhance the experience to share it with others.

4. **Stay Aware of Your Surroundings:** As with any beach or resort, it's wise to be aware of your environment. Keep personal belongings secure and be cautious of anyone acting suspiciously.

5. **Trust Your Instincts:** If a place feels uncomfortable or unwelcoming, it's okay to leave and seek another location.

6. **Respect Others' Privacy:** Nudist communities value consent and privacy. Always be respectful of others and avoid taking photos without permission.

And don't forget a towel!

 **General Questions**

1. *Are there specific beaches in Greece that are well-known for nudism, and what should I know before visiting them?* Yes. Paradise Beach and Seitan Limania are two of the most famous nudist beaches in Greece. Keep in mind that some beaches, such as Paradise Beach, are only accessible by boat.

2. *What should I wear when visiting a nude beach in Greece, and is it necessary to bring anything specific?* At a nude beach in Greece, you can choose to be completely nude or wear a bathing suit if you're not comfortable with nudity. Bring a towel or beach mat for hygiene and comfort, and don't forget sunscreen, especially if you'll be exposed to the sun for extended periods. It's also helpful to bring water, snacks, and a beach bag. Remember to dress if leaving the designated area, as public nudity outside these zones is not allowed.

 **Law of the Land Hypothetical**

HYPOTHETICAL: *Olivia, a French tourist, is planning to visit a beach in Greece and is wondering if it's acceptable to go topless on a regular, non-designated beach. What would happen if she went topless on a non-nude beach?"*

ANSWER: *While going topless is accepted in many parts of Europe, in Greece, it can be a bit more culturally sensitive depending on the location. On regular beaches (not designated for nudism), topless sunbathing is generally not illegal, but it may attract unwanted attention, and in some areas, it could be seen as disrespectful or inappropriate, especially in more conservative regions. In tourist-heavy areas, like Santorini or Mykonos, topless sunbathing is more common and usually tolerated. However, if you're in a smaller, more traditional village or less touristy areas, it's best to err on the side of caution and keep your top on. Always consider the local culture and the specific beach you're visiting.*

UNUSUAL LAWS

UNUSUAL LAWS

Overview

Unusual laws provide fascinating glimpses into a culture's values, historical evolution, and societal norms. While the majority of people are well aware of common legal restrictions, it is often the more eccentric and peculiar laws that tend to capture our attention. These laws, which can range from the amusing to the outright absurd, often reflect the distinctive circumstances, traditions, and unique historical events of a particular place. They can emerge from a wide array of sources, including past conflicts, shifting social expectations, or simply unusual local customs that have been passed down through generations.

What makes these laws particularly interesting is their ability to offer a deeper understanding of the cultural fabric that shapes a society. They provide a window into the mindset of a community, revealing how governance has adapted to historical, geographical, or social conditions. Furthermore, these unusual laws often serve as a reminder of how human behavior and legal systems are influenced by the ever-changing interplay of tradition, innovation, and cultural identity. Whether amusing or puzzling, such laws remain a testament to the quirky and diverse nature of human civilization.

Greece's Unusual Laws

Greece has its own fair share of unique laws and social quirks:

- Wearing high heels at certain ancient monuments is illegal. This law is designed to prevent damage to the historic sites, as sharp heels can cause erosion to the delicate stones.

- Like many European countries, Greece has laws regulating baby names, and parents can face restrictions on giving their children names that are deemed too foreign or bizarre. The Greek authorities prefer names that are consistent with Greek cultural and religious traditions. This is more of an official regulation than a quirky local law, but it's still a curious example of how naming practices are controlled by the state.

- Motorcycle helmets are mandatory for both drivers and passengers on motorcycles. However, in some cases, wearing a helmet while driving a car (specifically a sports car or a convertible) can result in fines, as it's considered a safety hazard or even a potential distraction to other drivers.

- While Greeks have a strong affection for animals, it is illegal to feed stray animals in certain places, particularly in tourist-heavy areas like Athens, as it can attract larger crowds of stray animals and negatively affect public health.

- It's against the law to wear a swimsuit or beachwear outside of designated swimming areas or beaches. So, even if you're just strolling down to the café in a tourist area, make sure to cover up with appropriate clothing.

- In Greece, divorce can be a tricky issue, especially in the context of inheritance laws. For example, a divorced person may not automatically inherit property from their former spouse unless there was an agreement before the divorce. These kinds of regulations vary, but they reflect Greece's unique handling of legal matters concerning personal relationships.

Penalties and Fines

The penalties for violating many of these laws can vary significantly, ranging from fines to arrest, and tourists are expected to adhere to the legal framework of Greece. Even seemingly minor infractions can lead to serious consequences, potentially placing a visitor in considerable legal trouble. In certain cases, breaches of local laws may result in expulsion from the country, substantial financial penalties, or even imprisonment. The severity of these penalties highlights the importance of understanding and respecting local regulations. Tourists should be particularly mindful that, regardless of how insignificant or obsolete a law may seem, failure to comply can lead to major legal repercussions.[72]

For example, when it comes to regulating baby names, parents who choose names that are considered too foreign or unusual by the authorities may face delays in the birth registration process. The name could be outright rejected, and parents might find themselves needing to go to court to challenge the decision. This can create significant administrative delays and add legal fees, especially if the parents are determined to keep the name despite the objections of the registry office.

In the case of wearing a swimsuit outside of designated areas, such as strolling through a café or town, the law prohibits it to maintain public decency. If caught, individuals can be fined anywhere from €50 to €100 (US$52 to $105). In addition to the financial penalty, they may be asked to leave the area or face uncomfortable social disapproval, especially in more conservative regions. This can result in a disrupted experience, particularly for tourists unaware of the local customs.

If caught feeding animals in Greece, you can face fines ranging from €100 to €300 (US$105 to $314). The law aims to prevent strays from gathering in large numbers, which can create hygiene issues and disrupt public spaces. This rule is enforced more strictly during tourist seasons, and businesses or individuals encouraging feeding may also face penalties.

---

72 https://www.countryreports.org/country/Greece/criminal-penalties.htm

? General Questions

1. *Is it illegal to wear camouflage clothing in Greece?* **Yes.** In Greece, it is illegal to wear camouflage clothing in public, except for the military, police, or security personnel. This law is primarily aimed at preventing civilians from impersonating military personnel, which could lead to confusion or security concerns. Those who violate this law may face fines or be asked to change their clothing. This rule is more strictly enforced in areas near military zones or during national holidays and events.

2. *What happens if I fail to pay a fine in Greece?* If you fail to pay a fine in Greece, you may face additional penalties or fines. Over time, authorities could take legal action to recover the money, which may include court proceedings or even asset seizure. For tourists, unpaid fines could prevent you from leaving the country, particularly for serious offenses. It's best to pay fines promptly or appeal them through legal channels to avoid complications.

3. *Are there any laws about taking photos in Greece?* **Yes.** There are laws about taking photos in Greece. While photography is generally allowed in public, it's prohibited in military zones and near military installations. Some museums and archaeological sites also restrict photography, particularly with flash. Additionally, you need consent to photograph people in private settings or situations where they expect privacy. Violating these rules can result in fines or being asked to delete the photos. Always check local signs for specific restrictions.

 **Law of the Land Hypothetical**

HYPOTHETICAL: *Maria, a tourist visiting Greece, is enjoying a day out in Athens when she decides to visit the Acropolis. She wears her favorite high heels to the site, not knowing the law about footwear at ancient monuments. While taking a photo of the Parthenon, she notices a sign prohibiting photography with a flash and sees several locals shaking their heads as she snaps a picture. As she walks through a nearby café, she realizes she forgot to cover up her swimsuit from the beach earlier and is now in the café in swimwear. What consequences might Maria face for her actions?*

ANSWER: *Maria could face several repercussions. First, for wearing high heels at the Acropolis, she may be asked to leave or fined, as the law aims to protect delicate historic stones from damage caused by sharp heels. Secondly, since photography is prohibited at certain sites like the Acropolis, Maria may be asked to delete her photos or face a fine if flash photography was used. Lastly, walking into a café in her swimsuit could result in a fine of €50 to €100 (US$52 to $105) for violating public decency laws, in addition to overt social disapproval. To avoid these issues, it's important for tourists to be aware of local customs and legal restrictions when visiting Greece.*

TRAVELING SAFELY

TRAVELING SAFELY

Ladies Traveling Solo

Greece is widely regarded as one of the safest destinations for tourists, with relatively few reports of violent crime targeting visitors. While the incidence of serious criminal activity is low, tourists may encounter instances of petty theft or pickpocketing, particularly in crowded areas or popular tourist destinations. However, these types of crimes are typically opportunistic in nature and can often be avoided with basic precautions. Overall, Greece remains a secure and welcoming environment for travelers.[73]

Greece is generally considered a safe destination for women traveling alone. The country is known for its friendly locals and vibrant culture, making it a popular spot for solo travelers. Major cities like Athens and Thessaloniki, along with tourist-heavy islands like Santorini and Mykonos, offer a safe and welcoming atmosphere.

Public transportation is safe, but it's best to avoid empty buses or trains late at night out of abundance of caution. Opting for reputable taxis or ride-hailing services adds an extra layer of security. Many tourist areas are particularly well-suited for solo travelers, and the overall relaxed Greek culture is easy to navigate, though it's advisable to dress modestly when visiting religious sites.

---

73 https://www.travelsafe-abroad.com/greece/

The challenges that solo female travelers often face tend to revolve around their personal safety and comfort. In many parts of the world, women traveling alone may encounter unwanted attention or feel uneasy in unfamiliar surroundings. However, in Greece, these issues are less frequent. While it is common for men to glance at or smile at women in passing, especially in social or tourist areas, it is rare for them to engage in intrusive behavior. Most interactions are brief, with a simple "hello" or a polite acknowledgment before they move on. This is particularly true on the Greek islands, where the atmosphere tends to be more relaxed and laid-back.

While solo women may occasionally feel uncomfortable walking around at night, particularly in less populated areas, they are generally safe as long as they avoid sketchy neighborhoods or poorly lit streets. Like in any destination, maintaining situational awareness and using common sense are key to staying safe. By taking simple precautions and being mindful of their surroundings, women traveling alone can confidently enjoy their time in Greece and experience all the country has to offer without significant concerns.[74]

It is advised that tourists exercise caution when visiting the smaller, more rural islands. These areas, often less developed for tourism, are home to many older generations and the residents generally prioritize their privacy and a quieter way of life, so visitors may find that the local environment is more reserved.

When visiting rural areas in Greece, it's important to be mindful of local customs. Dress modestly, especially in more conservative villages and religious sites, and avoid revealing clothing outside of the beach. Respect privacy and personal space, as rural communities tend to be more reserved. Politeness and formality are key, so greet people respectfully, often using titles like "Mr." or "Mrs." Life moves at a slower pace, so be patient with services and wait times. Respect traditions, especially if invited to a local home or event, and keep noise levels low to maintain the peaceful environment. Lastly, carry cash, as some rural businesses still prefer it over credit cards. Observing these norms will help ensure a respectful and enjoyable experience.

---

74 https://eatsleepbreathetravel.com/solo-travel-in-greece/

Safety Precautions for Female Solo Travelers[75]

- **Research your destination thoroughly:** Check current travel advisories and local news before visiting any area. Talk to the hotel or resort personnel or a trusted local about what areas to avoid.

- **Stick to well-populated areas:** Avoid venturing into isolated areas, especially at night. And always keep personal items close to the chest.

- **Use licensed taxis and ride-sharing services:** Be cautious about using street taxis and always confirm the route with the driver.

- **Inform someone of your plans:** Let a trusted friend or family member know your itinerary and expected return times.

- **Be aware of your surroundings:** Stay vigilant and trust your instincts.

- **Dress modestly in certain areas:** Depending on the region, dressing conservatively can help you avoid unwanted attention.

- **Learn basic Greek phrases:** Knowing a few basic Greek phrases can be helpful for communication.

The internet is a great resource for up-to-date tips and advice. Websites like **eatsleepbreathetravel.com/solo-travel-in-greece** offer excellent insights for female travelers heading to Greece. They provide valuable information on everything from safety tips, cultural etiquette, and practical travel advice, ensuring you have a smooth and enjoyable trip. Whether it's advice on navigating local customs, staying safe in different areas, or finding the best solo-friendly activities, such resources can be incredibly

---

75 https://wwwnc.cdc.gov/travel/destinations/traveler/none/greece

helpful for planning your journey and addressing any concerns you may have.

Traveling as a Family

When traveling with children, it's important to take proactive steps to ensure their safety and well-being before you even board the plane. Preparation goes beyond packing extra clothes and jackets; it's about planning how to monitor and protect your child in busy public spaces. Using safety tools like a tracking device, an ID tag with contact information, or a child safety alarm can provide peace of mind. These precautions help reduce the risk of separation or other safety issues, allowing parents to manage the stress of traveling and lessen the chances of any accidents or mishaps.

Health is a crucial consideration when traveling with children, particularly in busy destinations like Greece, which can have crowded tourist areas. It's important to ensure that children are up to date on all required vaccinations before the trip, as this prepares their immune systems for exposure to new environments and potential illnesses. Hygiene also plays a key role. Carrying hand sanitizer and teaching children the importance of frequent handwashing can help reduce the spread of germs. Parents should also guide their children on the proper handwashing techniques, especially after touching public surfaces. By taking these basic health precautions, parents can significantly reduce the risk of illness and focus on enjoying a safe, memorable trip with their children.

Advice for All Travelers

It's always wise to trust your instincts when assessing safety and stay within areas that feel secure and well-populated. Remain vigilant of your surroundings and avoid high-risk locations or situations that feel unsafe. Keeping your personal belongings secure is essential. Never leave drinks or food unattended and avoid letting unfamiliar individuals handle your items.

Ensure you have a fully charged phone and a backup power source, so you're always connected in case of an emergency. Carrying a reliable map can also help you navigate and stay aware of your surroundings, adding to your sense of security.

Equally important is maintaining respectful behavior throughout your stay. While Greece is known for its warm hospitality, disruptive or disrespectful actions can cause issues. Being mindful of local customs and etiquette will not only ensure a positive experience but also contribute to a harmonious atmosphere for both visitors and locals.[76]

Do's and Don'ts While in Greece

When visiting Greece, there are several important do's and don'ts to keep in mind for a smooth and respectful experience:

- **Do** dress modestly when visiting religious sites, such as churches and monasteries. Covering your shoulders and knees is considered respectful.

- **Don't** engage in loud or disruptive behavior, especially in smaller villages. Greece is known for its relaxed pace, and respect for quiet hours is important.

- **Do** greet people with a warm smile and a handshake, as Greeks are friendly and appreciate good manners.

- **Don't** take photos in places where it's prohibited, like certain museums or military zones. Always check for signs before snapping pictures.

- **Do** try the local food and drink. Greek cuisine is a highlight! Enjoy fresh seafood, tzatziki, and baklava.

---

76 https://www.ncesc.com/geographic-faq/
what-should-i-be-careful-of-in-greece/

- **Don't** tip excessively. While tipping is appreciated, it's not mandatory and should be modest (around 5-10% in restaurants).

- **Do** use public transportation or taxis to get around. It's affordable, efficient, and a great way to explore the country.

- **Don't** leave valuables unattended on the beach or in public areas. Petty theft can happen, especially in crowded tourist spots.

- **Do** take time to learn a few Greek phrases like "Kalimera" (Good morning) or "Efharisto" (Thank you). It shows respect for the local culture.

- **Don't** expect fast service in restaurants. Greek dining is often a leisurely, social experience, so be patient and enjoy the ambiance.

- **Do** respect personal space in public. Greeks value a sense of privacy, so avoid standing too close to others in queues or while waiting.

- **Don't** discuss sensitive political topics like the financial crisis or the country's past issues unless you're familiar with the person. It could lead to uncomfortable conversations.

- **Do** carry sunscreen, a hat, and water, especially in the summer months. Greece can get quite hot, and staying hydrated is key.

- **Don't** assume that everyone speaks English fluently, especially in rural areas. While many Greeks do understand English, learning a few basic Greek phrases or using translation apps can go a long way in making connections and showing respect for the local culture.

Engaging with the Locals

Interacting with locals in Greece is typically an easy and rewarding experience, as the Greek people are known for their warm hospitality. Even small efforts to engage with them are often met with appreciation. One great way to build rapport is by learning a few basic phrases in Greek, as it shows respect for the local language and culture. Greeks are generally grateful when visitors make this effort.

Greek cuisine is another integral part of the culture. Rooted in Mediterranean traditions, the diet focuses on fresh vegetables, olive oil, and exceptional seafood. Visitors can enjoy a wide range of healthy and flavorful dishes that highlight the region's rich culinary heritage.

Additionally, embracing local customs and traditions, such as participating in festivals and community events, is a fantastic way to connect with the locals. Greeks take great pride in their heritage and are eager to share it with visitors. By immersing yourself in these activities, you not only deepen your own experience but also build meaningful connections with the people of Greece.[77]

---

77 https://www.fixeringreece.com/blog/essen-
    tial-dos-and-don%E2%80%99ts-visitors-greece-navigating-local-cul-
    ture-and-etiquette-056

TOURIST TAXATION

- Overview
- Tourist Taxes in Greece
- Law of the Land Hypothetical

TOURIST TAXATION

Overview

Tourists in Greece are subject to taxes as part of the country's broader economic framework, which helps support both public services and the vital infrastructure. Greece relies heavily on tourism for economic stability, and taxes on goods, services, and accommodations play a crucial role in generating revenue. For example, the Value Added Tax (VAT) is an important source of national income, and as tourists enjoy local services, they contribute to the funding of essential services.

These taxes also ensure that Greece can maintain its public infrastructure, including transportation systems, healthcare, and emergency response services, all of which are used by both locals and visitors. By contributing through taxes, tourists help ensure that the country remains safe, efficient, and accessible for everyone.

Additionally, the funds generated from tourist taxes are used to preserve Greece's rich cultural heritage. With numerous ancient sites, museums, and landmarks scattered across the country, the revenue supports the upkeep, restoration, and protection of these iconic attractions, allowing future generations to appreciate them as well.

Ultimately, these taxes ensure that visitors pay their fair share for the services they enjoy during their stay—whether it's staying in hotels, dining at restaurants, using transportation, or exploring historical sites.

This system helps support the overall well-being of Greece, benefiting both its residents and its visitors.

Tourist Taxes in Greece

Tourists visiting Greece are subject to several types of taxes, which are typically included in the price of goods and services or collected at the point of purchase or service. Here's a breakdown of the main taxes tourists pay in Greece, how they are calculated, and paid:

1. Value Added Tax (VAT)

The VAT is a consumption tax applied to most goods and services in Greece, including food, clothing, and hotel accommodations.

The standard VAT rate is 24 percent, but there are reduced rates for specific items:

- 13 percent VAT for items like food in restaurants, public transport, and non-alcoholic beverages.
- 6 percent VAT for items such as books, theater tickets, and certain health-related products.

The VAT is typically included in the price of the product or service, meaning tourists usually don't need to pay it separately at the point of sale. It's already factored into the cost of hotel stays, restaurant meals, and most other purchases.

2. City Tax (Accommodation Tax)

This is a tax levied on tourists staying in hotels, guesthouses, or other accommodations. The tax is based on the rating of the accommodation:

- €0.5 per night (approximately US$0.55) for 1–2-star hotels
- €1.5 per night (approximately US$1.65) for 3-star hotels

- €3 per night (approximately US$3.30) for 4-star hotels
- €4 per night (approximately US$4.40) for 5-star hotels

This tax is usually paid directly to the hotel at check-in or check-out. It's not included in the accommodation's advertised price and is an additional charge.

3. Tourism and Municipality Taxes

In addition to VAT and city tax, some municipalities impose a small tourism tax on specific services, such as entry fees to cultural sites and museums.

The tax is generally a fixed amount, often a few euros per person for entry to museums, archaeological sites, or cultural events.

The tax is usually included in the entry fee for cultural attractions, so tourists don't need to pay it separately unless specified.

4. Airport/Departure Tax

Some airports in Greece charge a departure tax, which is included in the price of airline tickets.

This tax is generally calculated based on the flight's distance and the type of flight (domestic or international).

The departure tax is usually included in the price of the airline ticket, so passengers don't need to pay it separately at the airport.

5. Environmental Tax (Air Travel)

In some cases, Greece applies an environmental tax on tourists flying into the country as part of climate change mitigation efforts.

The tax is typically based on the distance between the departure point and Greece, with varying rates depending on the origin of the flight.

This tax is included in the airline ticket price, and the tax rate can vary depending on the departure city or country.

 **Law of the Land Hypothetical**

HYPOTHETICAL: *Sarah, an American tourist, arrives in Greece for a week-long vacation. After booking a 4-star hotel in Athens, she sees the room price advertised at €100 (US$105) per night. She also buys a ticket to visit the Acropolis and enjoys several meals at local restaurants. Upon check-out from her hotel, she is surprised to see an additional charge for €3 (US$3.15) per night labeled as "city tax." Additionally, when she purchases her entry ticket for the Acropolis, she notices a small fee added for "tourism tax." Confused, Sarah wonders if these extra charges are standard and why they weren't included in the initial price. Why did Sarah incur extra charges for the city tax and tourism tax during her stay in Greece?*

ANSWER: *The extra charges Sarah encountered are common tourist taxes in Greece. The city tax is a fixed fee based on the star rating of the hotel and is not included in the initial room rate. In Sarah's case, her 4-star hotel charges €3 (US$3.15) per night for this tax, which she pays separately at check-out. The tourism tax on her Acropolis ticket is a small fee added to the price of entry to cultural sites, helping fund the preservation of historical monuments and cultural heritage. These taxes are standard in Greece and are meant to support local infrastructure, public services, and environmental efforts, and are often paid directly at the point of purchase or service.*

LONG-TERM STAYS

CHAPTER 23

LONG-TERM STAYS

Overview

Greece has become an increasingly popular destination for foreign visitors seeking to stay long-term, drawn by its combination of natural beauty, cultural richness, and relatively affordable cost of living compared to other European countries. Many expats are attracted by the country's mild Mediterranean climate, which offers long, sun-drenched summers and mild winters, making it an ideal place for those who prefer outdoor living. Greece's diverse landscapes, from the serene beaches of the islands to the lush mountains in the mainland, offer a wide range of activities and a tranquil pace of life. For those in search of a more laid-back lifestyle, small villages and rural areas provide an escape from the bustle of city living, while larger cities like Athens and Thessaloniki offer vibrant cultural scenes and modern amenities.

In addition to the lifestyle benefits, Greece's rich history and cultural heritage are key factors for long-term visitors. Expats often find themselves captivated by the country's ancient ruins, iconic architecture, and traditional festivals that continue to shape Greek identity. Furthermore, Greece's strategic location within Europe offers easy access to other Mediterranean countries, making it an appealing base for travel. The relatively lower cost of living, especially outside major tourist areas, also makes it an attractive option for retirees, digital nomads, and those seeking to escape the higher costs associated with other Western European countries. With the added appeal of friendly locals and a welcoming environment, it's no wonder that many visitors are choosing to call Greece home for the long term.

Greece offers a range of ideal locations for long-term stays, each catering to different preferences. Athens and Thessaloniki provide vibrant city life with a mix of modern amenities and rich cultural experiences, perfect for those seeking an urban lifestyle. For a more serene and affordable lifestyle, Crete and the Peloponnese offer beautiful landscapes, a relaxed pace, and lower living costs, with Crete also providing excellent healthcare and a welcoming local community. The Ionian Islands and Cyclades are perfect for those desiring island living, with islands like Corfu, Kefalonia, and Naxos offering a quieter, more laid-back atmosphere. Rhodes and Mykonos provide a mix of rich history, stunning beauty, and vibrant international communities. Ultimately, Greece's diverse regions ensure there's a place for everyone, whether you seek city energy, island tranquility, or rural charm.

Living Costs

Living costs in Greece are generally lower than in many Western European and North American countries. Housing, groceries, and dining out tend to be more affordable, particularly outside major cities like Athens. Rent in Greek cities is much cheaper than in cities like London or Paris, with one-bedroom apartments in Athens costing around €400–€600 (US$440–$660). Groceries and eating out also cost less, with meals at casual restaurants typically around €10–€15 (US$11–$16). Utilities, transportation, and healthcare are similarly more affordable, with public transportation passes and utility bills being significantly lower than in cities like Berlin or New York. Overall, Greece offers a lower cost of living, especially in smaller towns and rural areas, making it an attractive destination for long-term stays.

Healthcare Options for Long-Term Visitors

For long-term visitors in Greece, healthcare options are both accessible and relatively affordable. Greece offers a public healthcare system, known as EOPYY, which provides essential medical services to residents and legal residents, including foreign nationals who have been living in the country for a certain period. Many long-term visitors opt for private health insurance, which ensures quicker access to private hospitals and doctors, often with a wider range of specialized services. Private health insurance plans in Greece are typically more affordable than in many Western countries, making them a popular choice for expats. Visitors can also pay directly for private care as needed, though this may be more expensive than public services.

Housing Options

Long-term visitors in Greece have a variety of housing options to choose from, depending on their preferences, budget, and desired location. Renting an apartment is one of the most common choices, with options ranging from modern, furnished apartments in major cities like Athens or Thessaloniki, to more traditional, spacious homes in rural areas or smaller towns. Rent can vary significantly based on location; in central areas of Athens, one-bedroom apartments typically cost between €400-€600 (US$420-$630) per month, while in less touristy or rural areas, rent can be as low as €300-€400 (US$315-$420).

For those looking for a more authentic experience, there are also villas and stone houses available for rent in the countryside or on islands like Crete or the Peloponnese, often at a higher price point, but offering more space and privacy. Shared accommodations, such as renting a room in a house or sharing an apartment, can also be an affordable option, especially for those on a tighter budget.

For visitors seeking short-term stays with more flexibility, Airbnb and other vacation rental platforms are widely available, but for long-term stays, securing a lease agreement with a local landlord is often the most cost-effective and stable solution.

Transportation Options

For long-term visitors in Greece, transportation options are varied and generally affordable, making it easy to navigate the country. In major cities, public transportation is a popular choice. The metro, buses, and trams are well-connected, reliable, and inexpensive, with monthly passes available for around €30-€40 (US$31.50–$42). These options are ideal for urban commuters and offer an efficient way to get around city centers. Taxis are also readily available but can be more expensive than public transport, though still relatively affordable compared to other European cities.

For those living outside major urban areas, regional trains and buses connect smaller towns and islands, though schedules can sometimes be less frequent. Car rentals are a convenient option for visitors who want flexibility, especially when traveling to more remote locations or exploring the countryside. Rental prices are reasonable, and driving in Greece is generally easy, though parking can be challenging in larger cities. Scooters and motorcycles are another popular choice for tourists and long-term visitors, especially in coastal areas or islands, offering a fun and practical way to get around.

For long-term stays, owning a car is an option, particularly if you plan to live in a more rural area, but you'll need to handle insurance, registration, and local driving requirements.

Language Considerations

Language can be an important consideration for long-term visitors in Greece. Although many Greeks, especially in tourist-heavy areas, speak English, the primary language is Greek. For those planning an extended stay, learning some basic Greek can be incredibly helpful, not only for daily interactions but also to show respect for the local culture. While younger generations and people working in tourism often have a good command of English, knowledge of Greek opens doors to richer, more meaningful interactions with locals, particularly in rural or less touristy areas where English may be less commonly spoken.

For everyday tasks like shopping, dealing with government paperwork, or navigating public services, understanding basic phrases can make life easier. Many long-term visitors take language courses or use language-learning apps to improve their skills. It's also common to see bilingual signs in major cities and tourist spots, but outside these areas,

Greek is overwhelmingly used in official documents, healthcare, and legal matters.

In terms of professional opportunities, knowing Greek can be a significant advantage for those seeking employment, as it increases access to more job options. While there are some jobs available in tourism, hospitality, or teaching English, fluency in Greek opens more avenues, particularly in fields like administration, education, or healthcare.

Long-Term Visas

For tourists planning to stay in Greece for an extended period, particularly those intending to remain for three months or longer, obtaining the appropriate visa is essential. Visitors who wish to stay in Greece for up to 90 days are generally advised to apply for a Schengen Visa, which grants access to Greece and other Schengen Area countries within the specified time frame. The Schengen Visa allows tourists to explore the country and the region, but it comes with the limitation of a 90-day stay within a 180-day period.

For those intending to stay in Greece for more than 90 days, a National Visa (also known as a D Visa) is required. This visa is issued for specific purposes such as employment, family reunification, higher education, or long-term residency. A National Visa allows visitors to stay in Greece for an extended period and is tailored to individuals who have more specific reasons for their stay, such as pursuing work opportunities, joining family members, or continuing their studies. Depending on the type of National Visa, the requirements and application processes can vary, so it is important for applicants to thoroughly review the specific criteria related to their intended purpose of stay. Here are some of the most common long-term visa options:

- **Residence Permit for Work:** This visa is designed for foreign nationals who secure employment in Greece. Applicants must have a job offer from a Greek employer, and the permit is typically tied to that specific employer. Work permits are issued for a limited duration and can be renewed. The requirements may vary depending on the type of work, but applicants often need to prove their qualifications and that no Greek or EU workers are available for the position.

- **Golden Visa (Investment Visa):** One of the most popular long-term visa options, the Greek Golden Visa allows non-EU nationals to obtain residence by making a qualifying investment. The most common route is through purchasing property worth at least €250,000 (US$262,500), although investments in other sectors, such as business or government bonds, can also qualify. The Golden Visa offers a residency permit for up to five years, with the possibility of renewal. It's particularly attractive because it allows the visa holder and their family to reside in Greece, with the ability to travel freely within the Schengen Zone.

- **Student Visa:** Foreign students who are accepted into a Greek educational institution can apply for a student visa. The visa is generally valid for the duration of their studies, and students are allowed to work part-time during their stay (up to 20 hours per week). To qualify, students must have proof of enrollment in an accredited Greek university or college, as well as sufficient financial means to support themselves during their stay.

- **Self-Employed or Freelance Visa:** Foreign nationals who wish to work as self-employed individuals or freelancers in Greece can apply for a residence permit for self-employed professionals. This is available to those in certain professions such as consultants, artists, and IT professionals, among others. Applicants must provide proof of their self-employment and show that they have sufficient income to support themselves.

- **Family Reunification Visa:** If a foreign national has a spouse, children, or other close family members legally residing in Greece, they can apply for a family reunification visa. This allows family members to join their relatives and live together in Greece. The applicant must provide proof of their family relationship and that the sponsor in Greece can support them financially.

- **Retirement Visa:** While Greece doesn't offer a specific "retirement visa," individuals who can demonstrate that they have a stable and sufficient income (such as pensions or other savings) may apply for a residence permit based on self-sufficiency. This is ideal for retirees who wish to live in Greece for an extended period without needing to work.

- **Entrepreneur Visa:** Entrepreneurs who plan to start a business in Greece can apply for a residence permit for business activities. The business must meet certain requirements, such as creating a certain number of jobs for Greek nationals or fulfilling other investment criteria. This visa is suitable for those who want to establish their own business in the country.[78]

 ## General Questions

1. *If I want to stay in Greece for long-term and work, should I apply for a work permit before arriving in Greece?* **Yes**. If you want to stay in Greece long-term and work, it's advisable to apply for a work permit before arriving. You typically need a job offer from a Greek employer, who must demonstrate they couldn't find a suitable candidate within Greece or the EU. Once you have the job offer, you can apply for a work visa at the Greek consulate or embassy in your home country. It's generally difficult to convert a tourist visa into a work visa while in Greece, so handling the process before arrival is recommended.

2. *I am American. Can I retire to Greece?* **Yes**. As an American, you can retire to Greece, but you'll need to meet certain requirements. Greece doesn't have a specific "retirement visa," but you can apply for a residence permit based on self-sufficiency. To qualify, you must prove that you have sufficient financial resources to support yourself without needing to work. This can include income from pensions, savings, or investments.

You'll also need to show that you have comprehensive health

---

78 https://www.expat.com/en/guide/europe/greece/35468-residence-permits-in-greece.html

insurance coverage, either private or through Greece's healthcare system. The permit is typically renewable and allows you to live in Greece long-term. It's a popular option for retirees seeking a high quality of life in a Mediterranean climate, with affordable living costs compared to other Western European countries. Make sure to consult with a Greek consulate for the latest requirements and application process.

 **Law of the Land Hypothetical**

HYPOTHETICAL: *Emily, an American retiree, has always dreamed of spending her golden years in Greece. After doing some research, she decides to apply for a long-term residence permit. Emily has a steady pension, savings, and private health insurance, but she's unsure if these meet the requirements for the visa. She wants to know if she can move to Greece permanently without needing to work.*

ANSWER: **Yes**, *Emily can retire to Greece with her pension and savings, as long as she can demonstrate she has enough financial resources to support herself without the need to work. The Greek government offers residence permits based on self-sufficiency, which is perfect for retirees. She will need to show proof of her pension income, savings, and private health insurance coverage. Emily should apply for the residence permit through the Greek consulate in her home country* **before** *arriving. Once granted, the permit will allow her to live in Greece long-term and is usually renewable. She should consult with the consulate to ensure she has all the required documentation and meets the latest criteria for the application.*

 ## Law of the Land True Story

Anthony Grant recounts an unexpected confrontation at Athens International Airport when he found himself caught up in the complexities of the Schengen Zone's visa rules. As a U.S. citizen, Grant had assumed that a brief trip to Cyprus would reset his 90-day stay limit in Greece. However, when he presented his passport at immigration, the officer pointed out that while Americans can stay in any Schengen country for up to 90 days within a 180-day period, the clock doesn't reset with a quick exit and re-entry. Grant had unknowingly overstayed his time in Greece, despite his attempt to stay within the limits, highlighting the confusion and importance of understanding the Schengen Area's intricate travel rules.[79]

 ## Takeaways

- Greece offers diverse living options, from vibrant cities like Athens to peaceful rural areas and islands, catering to various lifestyles.

- The cost of living in Greece is lower than in many Western countries, especially outside major cities, making it appealing for retirees and digital nomads.

- Greece's healthcare is affordable, with many expats opting for private insurance for quicker access to care, which is generally cheaper than in other Western nations.

- Greece provides several long-term visa options, including work, student, self-employed, and investment visas. The Golden Visa, based on real estate investment, is particularly popular.

- While many Greeks speak English in tourist areas, learning Greek is recommended for cultural integration, better communication, and more job opportunities.

---

79 https://thepointsguy.com/travel/schengen-zone-visa-rules/

CIVIL LITIGATION

CIVIL LITIGATION

Overview

Civil litigation provides a mechanism for resolving disputes, ensuring that travelers have a way to seek justice if legal issues arise while visiting another country. It helps them understand their rights and obligations under local laws, which may differ from those in their home country. The civil litigation system offers a formal process for addressing conflicts, such as contract disputes or personal injury claims, and can deter unfair practices by encouraging businesses to comply with legal standards. It also allows individuals to seek financial recourse for damages or losses and helps protect them from potential exploitation by local entities. Overall, understanding civil litigation enhances a visitor's experience and safety while traveling.

Personal Injury Claims and Compensation Law

In Greece, there are several grounds on which a person can file a personal injury claim. One of the most common scenarios involves traffic accidents. If a tourist or resident is injured in a road traffic accident caused by another driver's negligence, they are entitled to seek compensation. The same holds true for workplace accidents, where employees who suffer injuries due to unsafe working conditions or employer negligence have the right to file a claim for damages.

Accidents that occur within educational institutions also provide grounds for a claim. For instance, if a student is injured due to negligent supervision or unsafe facilities in a school or university, they can pursue compensation. In addition, accidents stemming from contractual and tortious liability—such as those caused by faulty services or products— are valid reasons for filing a claim. For example, if a service provider's failure to uphold safety standards results in injury, the victim can seek redress.

Lastly, injuries that happen in public spaces or on private property— such as hotels, restaurants, or shops—are also grounds for compensation. These could occur due to poorly maintained facilities, hazardous conditions, or negligence on the part of the property owner. Whether a person is harmed on the road, at work, in an educational setting, or in any other circumstance where negligence is involved, the Greek legal system offers a path for seeking justice and compensation.

What to Do If You Get Injured

In the unfortunate event of an injury while visiting Greece, filing an injury claim is essential to ensure that victims receive the compensation they deserve. However, the claims process requires specific documentation and evidence to build a strong case. Understanding the required steps and having the appropriate documentation can help streamline the process and ensure a smoother resolution.

The primary documentation required for filing a claim is the official paperwork that outlines the details of the incident. Alongside this paperwork, it is critical to provide photographic evidence of the accident, including pictures of the damage and any visible injuries. This documentation serves as vital proof to support the claims and clarify the circumstances surrounding the incident.

In the case of a car accident, additional documentation is required. This includes not only the personal information of both parties involved in the accident but also details about the vehicles, such as registration and insurance information. It is also essential to collect information regarding any injuries sustained by the other party that may have contributed to or resulted from the accident. Furthermore, eyewitness accounts from individuals who witnessed the incident can significantly strengthen the claim by corroborating the victim's version of events. Eyewitness testimonies provide crucial third-party validation, making them invaluable for the claims process.

It is also important to note that filing an injury claim in Greece must be done within 30 days of the accident. If the claim is not submitted within this time frame, it is no longer valid, and the victim forfeits the opportunity to seek compensation. Therefore, it is crucial to act promptly and submit all necessary documentation within the designated time frame to ensure eligibility for compensation.

The calculation of damages following an accident is typically based on three main factors: the physical damage to property, the physical injuries sustained by the victim as a result of the accident, and finally the emotional or psychological damage caused by the incident. Compensation for these damages is typically shared between the government and the party found responsible for causing the accident.

In addition to the compensation from the government and the at-fault party, insurance often plays a significant role in covering the costs associated with the accident. Insurance coverage typically includes both the damage to property and the initial medical expenses incurred from immediate care following the incident. Having comprehensive insurance coverage can reduce the financial burden on the victim and expedite the compensation process.

Legal fees are another consideration in the claims process. In many cases, a lawyer may be required to assist with the claim, particularly if the responsible party contests the allegations. Legal fees are typically agreed upon in advance, and lawyers generally receive a percentage of the final compensation amount, often around 33 percent. This means that the lawyer's payment is contingent on the successful resolution of the case.

While the injury claims process in Greece can be challenging, with potential obstacles such as uncooperative police, insufficient evidence, or insurance companies refusing to cover certain damages, the effort is often worthwhile. Even if the compensation amount is modest, it can provide significant relief in the aftermath of an accident. The legal system in Greece is generally cooperative, and most cases are resolved fairly, with compensation provided to help the victim recover and move forward.[80]

How to File a Civil Claim

In Greece, several courts play distinct roles in addressing civil matters. The Court of the Peace, the Single-Member Court of First Instance, and the Small Claims Court each handle specific types of civil disputes. These courts work together to resolve issues and restore peace between parties involved in legal conflicts. Understanding which court handles your specific case is crucial, as each court has its jurisdiction based on the nature and value of the claim.

When filing a civil claim in Greece, tourists must follow a specific process to ensure their case is properly presented and handled by the Greek legal system. The process typically begins by seeking assistance from the home embassy, as they can provide valuable guidance and support. Once the paperwork is completed (in Greek), it must be submitted to a district civil court. After filing the initial action document, it's crucial to provide pleadings, documents, and evidence that support the claim against the responsible party. These materials help the court gain a thorough understanding of the case. Once everything is submitted, a court date will be set, and the dispute will be resolved in the appropriate court based on the details of the case.

In addition to the procedural requirements, there are fees associated with filing a civil dispute in Greece. Currently, the court fees for submitting a civil case can amount to up to US$350, depending on the specifics of the case. These fees must be paid before the claim can be processed and considered by the court.[81]

80 https://generisonline.com/understanding-the-claims-process-and-dispute-resolution-mechanisms-in-greece/

81 https://undisputedlegal.com/greece-code-of-civil-procedure/

Service of Documents

One of the primary requirements is that all documents must be submitted in Greek, ensuring clarity and uniformity in legal proceedings across the country. Furthermore, the service of these documents is still carried out by court bailiffs, who are legal personnel with specific authority in the courtroom. This process ensures that the delivery of legal documents adheres to formalities and maintains a high standard of accountability. Once service has been carried out, proof of service must be filed with the court to confirm that the documents have been properly delivered to the intended parties. The recipient may be asked to sign a confirmation of receipt, which serves as proof of service. If the document cannot be personally handed over, the court will be notified of the failed attempt, and further steps will be taken to complete the service.

Documents in Greece can be served either in person at the court or electronically, depending on the nature of the case and the specific procedures required. Regardless of the method, both options are overseen and reviewed by a court official to ensure that proper protocol is followed. For international cases, documents can be served via diplomatic channels or the Hague Convention on the Service Abroad of Judicial and Extrajudicial Documents. This ensures that foreign nationals or entities involved in a legal case can be notified of legal actions.

In practice, service of legal documents is often conducted by bailiffs. These professionals have been granted the authority to serve and review documents on behalf of the court. Their role extends beyond simple delivery, as they are responsible for managing the entire process of serving documents, ensuring that all legal requirements are met. Their duties are directed by the person overseeing the court proceeding, ensuring that the service process is conducted in accordance with the law and that no steps are overlooked.

The proof of service is documented directly through the court system. It is the court's responsibility to ensure that all relevant documents are filed, tracked, and accounted for. Once proof of service has been established, the court can make copies of the relevant documents and send them to the necessary parties as directed by the case's proceedings.[82]

Statute of Limitations

In Greece, the statute of limitations refers to the legal time limit within which a party can file a lawsuit or initiate a legal action. Once this period expires, the claim can no longer be legally pursued, regardless of its merit. The length of the statute of limitations can vary depending on the type of claim and the specific circumstances of the case.

For example, in **personal injury claims**, the statute of limitations is generally **five years** from the date of the injury. However, for **contractual claims**, the period is usually **five years** as well, while **claims related to property damage** may have a limitation of **ten years**. Different rules apply to specific types of cases, such as commercial disputes or inheritance matters, where time frames can range from **one to twenty years**. The exact duration is influenced by factors like the nature of the claim (civil, criminal, etc.), the parties involved (individuals, government, corporations), and whether the claim involves any public interest or special regulations.[83]

If a lawsuit is filed after the statute of limitations has expired, the defendant can raise the expiration of the limitation period as a defense. If the court accepts this argument, the claim will be dismissed, and the plaintiff will not be able to seek compensation or relief. However, **exceptions** exist that can extend or suspend the statute of limitations in certain situations. For example:

1. **Minority or Incapacity:** If the claimant is a minor or legally incapacitated, the statute of limitations may be suspended until they reach the age of majority or regain their legal capacity.

---

82 https://stellarkonsulting.com/international-process-service/greece/

83 https://e-justice.europa.eu/279/EN/
    time_limits_on_procedures?GREECE&member=1

2. **Fraud or Concealment:** If the defendant fraudulently concealed the facts underlying the claim (e.g., hiding evidence or deliberately misinforming the plaintiff), the limitation period may be extended.

3. **Force Majeure:** If an external event (such as war, natural disasters, or pandemics) makes it impossible for the claimant to pursue legal action, the statute of limitations may be suspended during the period of impossibility.

Thus, while the statute of limitations is a critical time frame for filing claims, there are several factors and exceptions that may alter its length or provide opportunities for an extension. It's important for individuals to understand these provisions and seek legal advice if they believe their claim may be impacted by such rules.

 **Getting Married in Greece**[84]

Marriage in Greece is an attractive option for many international couples, drawn to the country's scenic beauty and cultural richness. While residency or citizenship is not required to marry in Greece, there are specific legal requirements, especially when one party is a Greek citizen or resident. In such cases, the Greek national must have a valid residence permit. Both parties must also present valid identification documents, like passports or national IDs.

If a foreign national is marrying a Greek citizen, they must provide a valid residence permit and submit a certified, translated birth certificate. A Certificate of No Impediment (CNI) from the foreign national's home country may also be required. This certificate, confirming that no legal barriers exist to the marriage, must be legalized and translated into Greek.

To apply for a marriage license in Greece, the necessary documents, including a marriage certificate from the Greek Consulate and valid

---

84 https://thewhiteedit.com/greece/

identification, must be submitted within 40 days of the planned wedding. The legal minimum age for marriage in Greece is 18, aligning with the age of consent. Individuals under 18 cannot legally marry.

The marriage can be registered either by one of the parties or by someone with a signed power of attorney from a Notary Public. The registration process is typically completed within three business days, and the official marriage certificate will be available for collection shortly thereafter.

Couples planning to marry in Greece have the option to choose between a civil and religious ceremony. A **civil ceremony** is a legally binding marriage without religious elements, while a **religious ceremony** follows the traditions of the couple's faith but is equally valid legally. The type of ceremony does not affect the legal validity of the marriage, allowing couples to select the option that best aligns with their personal beliefs and preferences.

In terms of legal and administrative **costs**, couples should expect certain fees. The affidavit of marriage typically costs around €7 (US$7.41), while the documentation required for the marriage ranges from 200 to €500 (US$211.58 to $528.95). If translation services are needed for documents like the Certificate of No Impediment or birth certificates, these can cost around €100 (US$105.79).

Before marrying in Greece, couples should verify that their marriage will be legally recognized in their home country. Some countries may not acknowledge foreign marriages unless certain legal requirements, such as document translations, are fulfilled. To avoid complications, it's essential for couples to check their home country's regulations regarding the recognition of foreign marriages. Additionally, couples may need to register their marriage with local authorities and provide personal information before finalizing any wedding plans. This step ensures that the marriage is legally valid both in Greece and in their home country.

 **Law of the Land Hypothetical**

HYPOTHETICAL: *Liam, an Irish tourist, was involved in a car accident in Greece in 2020. Although he wasn't badly injured, he did hit his head during the collision. After visiting a local doctor, no serious issues were identified, and Liam decided not to pursue any legal action against the person responsible for the accident. However, in 2024, Liam started experiencing persistent headaches and was informed by his doctor that he might begin suffering seizures as a result of the head injury from the crash. The only documented head injury on file is from the 2020 accident in Greece. Liam wants to take legal action against the responsible party, but he's concerned that the statute of limitations for filing a claim has expired, leaving him uncertain about his options for seeking compensation. What should he do?*

ANSWER: *Liam may still have options despite the statute of limitations potentially expiring. In Greece, personal injury claims typically have a three-year limit from the date of the injury or its discovery. Since Liam's symptoms became serious only in 2024, he may be able to argue that the statute of limitations starts from when the injury was diagnosed, not from the 2020 accident.*

To explore this possibility, Liam should consult a local Greek attorney specializing in personal injury law. The lawyer can assess whether any exceptions apply, such as delayed symptoms or hidden injuries, and help Liam gather medical records that link his current condition to the 2020 accident. Liam should seek legal advice as soon as possible to fully understand his options and the best path forward.

CHAPTER 25

OTHER THINGS TO KNOW

IN THIS CHAPTER

- Tourists and Street Hustling
- Safety Concerns and Practical Tips
- In the Event of Death
- Experiencing Financial Hardship

OTHER THINGS TO KNOW

Tourists and Street Hustling

Street hustling is a challenge that many tourists encounter when visiting Greece. Common tactics employed by street hustlers aim to deceive or pressure unsuspecting tourists into spending money on goods, services, or experiences that may not be as they seem. These hustlers often operate in high-traffic tourist areas, taking advantage of crowds to make quick profits. Below are some common tactics, goods, and services offered by street hustlers, as well as the areas in Greece where these activities are most prevalent.

Street hustling is particularly prevalent in some of Greece's most popular tourist hotspots, where the high volume of visitors makes it easier for hustlers to target unsuspecting tourists. In Athens, areas like Monastiraki Square, Plaka, and around the Acropolis are frequent spots for street vendors and scam artists, offering everything from fake souvenirs to overpriced services. Santorini, with its stunning views and bustling towns like Fira and Oia, also sees a fair share of hustlers, often approaching tourists with "free" gifts or trying to sell overpriced tours. The party island of Mykonos is another hotspot, especially in Mykonos Town, where tourists are targeted with fake entry tickets to clubs or overcharged drinks at bars. On the island of Crete, in places like Heraklion and Chania, hustlers often sell counterfeit goods or trick visitors into paying too much for boat tours or excursions. Similarly, Rhodes, Corfu, and other well-trodden islands are not immune, with vendors and scam artists often targeting tourists in busy areas like Rhodes Old Town or Corfu Town. In these areas, tourists should be extra cautious, as street hustling tactics are designed to take advantage of their unfamiliarity with the region.

Common tactics include offering "free" gifts or trinkets that later come with a hefty price, selling overpriced or fake souvenirs, and posing as official guides or charity collectors to pressure tourists into giving money. Scammers also offer fake tickets or discounted tours, overcharge for taxi rides, and engage in rigged street gambling games. Some even run bait-and-switch schemes at restaurants or offer unlicensed services like boat rides and parking, leaving tourists with inflated bills or unreliable transportation. Travelers should stay alert, avoid deals that seem too good to be true, and verify the legitimacy of any offers to protect themselves from these common scams.[85]

Safety Concerns and Practical Tips

Street hustling, in the sense of scams and fraudulent activities targeting tourists, is illegal in Greece, as it is in most countries. The Greek legal system prohibits deceptive practices such as misleading advertising, fraud, and the manipulation of tourists into paying inflated or bogus fees for goods and services. However, the enforcement of laws against street hustlers can sometimes be inconsistent, particularly in areas heavily frequented by tourists, such as Athens, Thessaloniki, and the popular islands. In these high-traffic tourist zones, the sheer number of people and the transient nature of visitors can make it more difficult for authorities to effectively regulate or catch offenders.

How to Avoid Street Hustling

To avoid falling victim to street hustling in Greece, tourists can take several precautions. The best way to protect yourself from these situations is to avoid engaging with street hustlers altogether. If you spot someone who seems to be trying to push a sale or force a service on you,

---

85 https://travelhiatus.com/9-scams-in-greece-to-watch-out-for/

walk away calmly and confidently. It's also helpful to avoid making eye contact with such individuals, as this can sometimes encourage them to approach you.

If you do encounter a hustler, be cautious of unsolicited offers or interactions from strangers, especially in busy tourist areas like Athens' Plaka district, the islands, or at popular landmarks. These are common hotspots for hustlers. If an offer seems too good to be true, it probably is.

Avoid engaging in deals with street vendors who don't have clear prices or those who approach you aggressively. If you do purchase anything, ensure that you know the price upfront and insist on a receipt for any transactions. Also, be wary of "friendly" individuals who may offer you directions or assistance in exchange for a tip or a "favor," which can often end up being a scam.

Always use reputable services, whether it's for transportation (e.g., licensed taxis) or activities (e.g., organized tours). It's safer to book tours or experiences through established companies or your hotel. Finally, stay alert to your surroundings and trust your instincts. If a situation feels uncomfortable or suspicious, walk away and avoid further interaction. Seek out a more public area where there are plenty of local residents. Greek locals, particularly older individuals, often have a strong sense of community and are typically willing to intervene when they notice a scammer trying to exploit a tourist. These locals are more likely to stand up to the hustler and diffuse the situation, which can offer some protection and peace of mind. If the issue escalates, involve the police![86]

---

86   https://www.travelnguides.com/is-greece-safe/

 ## In the Event of Death[87]

In the unfortunate event of a death while traveling in Greece, there are several important steps and procedures to follow to ensure the proper handling of the deceased's remains, as well as the necessary legal documentation. The process can be overwhelming, but understanding the steps involved can help ease some of the burden during such a difficult time.

The first critical step is obtaining a **medical certificate of** death within 24 hours of the passing. This certificate must be issued by a licensed Greek doctor and confirms the cause and time of death. Afterward, the certificate should be taken to the local Registry Office (Municipal Office) in the area where the deceased was staying to officially register the death. This will allow the issuance of an official death certificate, which is necessary for any further actions, such as burial or repatriation of the body.

If a tourist passes away in Greece, the family or accompanying person should call the **emergency number 166** to report the death. Local authorities will arrive at the scene to handle the body and transport it to the appropriate medical facility. From there, the family will be updated on the situation and can begin making decisions regarding the deceased's remains. Local medical personnel will also assist with the paperwork required for legal purposes.

To report the death and register it, the following documents will be needed:

- The Greek passport or ID card of the deceased.
- The passport or ID card of the person reporting the death (the informant).
- A certificate of municipal registration in Greece, issued within the last six months.

---

87 https://greece.refugee.info/en-us/articles/4985615467671

▪ A medical certificate of death signed by a licensed doctor.

These documents ensure that the death is officially recorded and that the necessary legal processes can continue.

Once the death certificate is issued, the family can decide whether to proceed with burial in Greece or repatriate the remains. The deceased can be buried in Greece, and funeral homes in the area will handle the logistics of burial. Local funeral homes can arrange for viewing, ceremony, and burial at a cemetery. If the family prefers to return the deceased's body to their home country, repatriation will involve several steps:

▪ Obtaining a permit from the local health department to transport the body, ensuring it meets health and safety standards.

▪ The body must be embalmed and placed in a hermetically sealed casket to prevent the spread of disease.

▪ Necessary health and legal documents (such as the death certificate and health permits) must accompany the remains during transport.

▪ Customs clearance is required for the international transport of the body, and the repatriation service must comply with both Greek and international regulations.

In the event of a death abroad, the embassy or consulate of the deceased's home country plays a vital role in assisting the family through the legal and logistical complexities of handling the situation. They act as intermediaries, communicating with local authorities on behalf of the family to ensure all necessary procedures are followed. The embassy also provides guidance and, in some cases, financial assistance to cover the costs of repatriation or funeral arrangements. If the family decides to repatriate the body, the embassy can help arrange the transport or, alternatively, assist with organizing a local burial in Greece. Additionally, the embassy ensures that all required documentation, including the Consular Report of Death, is completed, making certain that the legal requirements in both Greece and the home country are met efficiently.

Experiencing Financial Hardship

Tourists in Greece may face financial hardship for various reasons, including overspending on accommodation, food, and entertainment, especially in popular tourist areas. Emergencies like medical issues, accidents, or theft of valuables can lead to unexpected expenses. Currency exchange fees, travel delays, and hidden ATM charges also contribute to financial strain. Additionally, insufficient travel insurance or lack of understanding about the local insurance system can leave tourists vulnerable to high costs.

If you find yourself in financial hardship while traveling in Greece, there are several steps you can take and resources available to help you through the situation:

- **Contact Your Embassy or Consulate:** The embassy or consulate of your home country can provide essential support. They may assist in emergencies, such as arranging emergency funds, helping with repatriation, or offering guidance on accessing financial assistance. They can also liaise with local authorities on your behalf if necessary.

- **Reach Out to Your Bank or Credit Card Company:** Many banks offer emergency services, such as temporary card replacements or emergency funds transfer. If you're facing issues with your bank account or card, contacting your bank might resolve the problem quickly.

- **Seek Assistance from Local Charities or NGOs:** Various organizations in Greece offer help to tourists facing financial difficulties. These groups can provide information on local support programs, food, shelter, or even emergency financial aid. Some tourist areas have visitor centers that can direct you to these resources.

- **Contact Your Travel Insurance Provider:** If you have travel insurance, reach out to your provider immediately. Many travel insurance policies offer emergency financial assistance, covering things like medical costs, lost baggage, or trip delays. They might also help facilitate a transfer of funds if needed.

- **Explore Short-Term Loan or Emergency Cash Services:** If you urgently need cash, local payday loan services or money transfer providers like Western Union can offer quick cash transfers, though it's important to be mindful of interest rates and fees.

- **Consider Changing Your Travel Plans:** If your situation is dire, consider cutting short your trip or altering your travel plans. Opting for more budget-friendly accommodations, transportation, or eating in less tourist-heavy areas may help you manage expenses better.

- **Local Community and Social Media:** In some cases, local communities or social media platforms (such as local Facebook groups or travel forums) might offer helpful advice or even direct assistance from other travelers or residents who are familiar with the area.

As always, your home embassy is a crucial resource. The American Embassy in Greece can assist travelers facing financial hardship by providing emergency financial guidance, facilitating wire transfers, and helping arrange repatriation if needed. They can contact your family or friends to arrange emergency funds, issue emergency travel documents if lost, and refer you to local resources for additional support. While they don't offer direct financial assistance, the embassy plays a crucial role in helping tourists navigate financial challenges and access the necessary help to resolve their situation.

QUICK REFERENCE GUIDE

- Quick Chapter References to Important Topics

QUICK REFERENCE GUIDE

Crime in Greece

Are there particular areas I should avoid as a tourist?

Yes. While Greece is generally safe for tourists, areas like Omonia and Exarchia in Athens, as well as crowded tourist spots like Plaka and Monastiraki, can be prone to pickpocketing and scams. It's best to stay vigilant in busy areas and avoid walking alone late at night in unfamiliar districts. Most of Greece is safe, but being mindful of your belongings and surroundings is key. *For more details, see Chapter 3.*

Drug Offenses

Is the possession of marijuana legal?

No. The possession of marijuana is illegal in Greece. While there has been some discussion about decriminalization for small amounts for personal use, it remains illegal. Possession, trafficking, and cultivation of marijuana can result in criminal charges, with penalties ranging from fines to imprisonment, depending on the quantity involved.

Is the possession of cocaine legal?

No. The possession of cocaine is illegal in Greece. It is classified as a controlled substance, and being caught with cocaine can lead to serious legal consequences, including imprisonment. Greece has strict drug laws, and trafficking or possession of any illegal drug is treated severely. *For more details, see Chapter 4.*

Alcohol-Related Offenses

What is the legal drinking age?

The legal drinking age in Greece is **18 years old.**

What is the legal blood alcohol limit to drive?

The legal blood alcohol concentration (BAC) limit for drivers is:

- **0.05% (0.5 grams per liter of blood)** for regular drivers.
- **0.02% (0.2 grams per liter of blood)** for drivers with less than two years of experience and professional drivers (e.g., taxi drivers, truck drivers, etc.).

If you're caught driving with a BAC above the legal limit, you could face fines, license suspension, and even imprisonment, depending on the severity of the offense. It's always safest to avoid drinking and driving altogether. *For more details, see Chapter 5.*

Firearm & Ammunition Offenses

Can I possess a gun?

Yes. However, in Greece, gun ownership is strictly regulated. You can possess a firearm only if you meet specific requirements, such as being over 18, passing a background check, and having a valid reason (e.g., hunting, sports shooting). A license is required to own a gun and carrying it in public is generally prohibited unless explicitly authorized.

Can I possess ammunition?

Yes. Possessing ammunition is also regulated, and you need a separate license for it. Unauthorized possession of a firearm or ammunition can lead to severe penalties. *For more details, see Chapter 6.*

Prostitution

Is prostitution legal?

> **Yes.** Prostitution is legal in Greece, but it is regulated. Sex workers must be registered, undergo health checks, and work in licensed brothels. Public solicitation and trafficking are illegal. *For more details, see Chapter 7.*

LGBTQ

Is homosexuality legal?

> **Yes.** Homosexuality is legal in Greece. Same-sex relationships are not only legal but are also recognized under Greek law. In 2015, Greece legalized civil unions for same-sex couples, providing many of the same legal rights as marriage, although full marriage rights were granted later in some regions.

Are same-sex public displays of affection legal?

> **Yes.** Same-sex public displays of affection are legal as well. Greece is generally tolerant toward LGBTQ+ individuals, particularly in larger cities like Athens and Thessaloniki. However, as with many places, public reactions may vary in more rural or conservative areas. Nonetheless, the legal framework protects individuals against discrimination based on sexual orientation. *For more details, see Chapter 8.*

Arrested in Greece

Would I be entitled to bail if I'm arrested?

> If you're arrested in Greece, you are entitled to bail, but it depends on the severity of the crime and whether the court considers you a flight risk or a danger to the public. For minor offenses, you might be granted bail, but for more serious crimes, you may be held in detention until your trial.

Will a lawyer be provided to me if I cannot afford one?

Yes. If you cannot afford a lawyer, Greece provides public defenders (also called "court-appointed lawyers") for individuals who cannot afford to hire one. These lawyers will be appointed to represent you in criminal cases, ensuring that your right to legal counsel is upheld, in line with the country's legal system. *For more details, see Chapter 10.*

Helping a Friend or Relative Imprisoned in Greece

Can I send money to a friend or relative imprisoned in Greece?

Yes. You can send money to a friend or family member imprisoned in Greece. Funds can be deposited into the prisoner's account, usually through a bank transfer or by other means specified by the particular correctional facility. It is essential to check with the specific prison or detention center for the approved methods of sending money, as the procedures may vary.

Can I remain in Greece upon release from prison or jail after my sentence is complete?

Yes. You can remain in Greece after serving your sentence, provided you have legal permission to stay in the country. If you're a foreign national, you may need to ensure your visa or residency status is valid for continued stay after your release. If you do not have the proper residency status or visa, you may be required to leave the country. It's important to check with Greek immigration authorities to confirm the conditions of your stay following your release. *For more details, see Chapter 12.*

Crime Victim Assistance

Can a victim of a crime be legally compensated?

Yes. Victims of crime in Greece can be legally compensated under certain circumstances. Victims may be entitled to compensation for physical injury, emotional distress, and property damage caused by a crime. The compensation is typically provided by the Greek state through a victim support fund, particularly in cases where the perpetrator cannot be identified or is unable to pay damages. Victims can also seek compensation through civil litigation, where they can pursue claims for damages directly against the offender.

Does the Greece government offer assistance for family members of homicide victims?

Yes. The Greek government offers assistance to the family members of homicide victims. This support may include financial compensation, particularly if the victim's family members are facing economic hardship due to the loss. Additionally, family members can access psychological support and counseling services through victim-support programs. These services aim to help grieving families cope with the trauma and legal proceedings following the loss of a loved one due to homicide. *For more details, see Chapter 14.*

U.S. Consulate Assistance

Are there any limitations to the consulate assistance I can receive while in Greece?

Yes. Consular assistance in Greece is limited in certain areas. While consulates can help with legal documentation, emergencies, and repatriation, they cannot intervene in local legal matters or provide financial support beyond emergencies. They also cannot offer legal representation or help resolve private disputes. Additionally, consulates cannot act outside the bounds of Greek law or take over criminal investigations. *For more details, see Chapter 14.*

Police

Is there an official police force?

Yes. Greece has an official national police force known as the **Hellenic Police.** This force is responsible for maintaining law and order throughout the country. It handles a wide range of duties, including crime prevention, traffic control, investigations, border security, and counter-terrorism efforts. Local police forces in municipalities and regional divisions operate under the umbrella of the Hellenic Police. *For more details, see Chapter 15.*

How to Get Legal Help in Greece

Is there a resource in Greece to find legal representation?

Yes. In Greece, you can find legal representation through the local Bar Association, which is the governing body for lawyers. Each city has its own local bar association, and they provide directories of licensed lawyers across various specialties. You can also search for lawyers online or ask for recommendations from locals, embassies, or consulates.

Is there free legal representation assistance?

Yes. Greece provides free legal aid for individuals who meet financial and social criteria. To qualify, you must demonstrate a low income. Free legal aid is typically available for serious criminal cases, civil matters like family law, or when fundamental rights are at risk. Some NGOs also offer pro bono legal assistance to specific groups, such as refugees or low-income individuals. *For more details, see Chapter 16.*

Foreign Embassies in Greece

Are there foreign embassies in Greece?

Yes. Greece hosts numerous foreign embassies, particularly in Athens, where most diplomatic missions are located. These embassies provide services to their citizens, including assistance with legal, consular, and emergency matters.

Is there a website to locate embassies in Greece?

Yes. You can visit the official website of the Ministry of Foreign Affairs of Greece to find a list of foreign embassies and consulates in the country. Additionally, websites like **EmbassyPages** and **ConsulateFinder** offer comprehensive directories of diplomatic missions worldwide, including in Greece. *For more details, see Chapter 16.*

Medical Facilities & Hospitals

Is there a number I can call for ambulance and fire emergencies?

Yes. In Greece, you can call **112** for emergency services, including ambulances and fire emergencies. This number is part of the EU-wide emergency response system.

If I am injured while on vacation in Greece, are there hospitals that are recommended for tourists?

Yes. Major cities like Athens and Thessaloniki have hospitals that are well-equipped to handle emergencies and provide services to tourists. Some hospitals, like **Attikon University Hospital** in Athens, are known for treating international patients. Additionally, many hospitals and clinics in tourist areas, such as Crete and the Greek Islands, offer services in English and are familiar with the needs of foreign visitors. It's always advisable to check if the hospital has international patient services or an English-speaking staff. *For more details, see Chapter 17.*

Driving in Greece

Which side of the road do I drive on?

In Greece, you drive on the **right side** of the road.

Can I use my driver's license from my home country to drive in Greece?

Yes. Tourists can use their **foreign driver's license** to drive in Greece for up to **six months**. It's advisable to carry an **International Driving Permit** (**IDP**) along with your national driver's license for easier communication, especially if your license is not in English or Greek.

How old do I need to be to rent a car?

To rent a car in Greece, the minimum age is generally **21**. However, some rental companies may have higher age requirements, especially for luxury or larger vehicles. Drivers under 25 may also be subject to a young driver fee. *For more details, see Chapter 18.*

Nude Beaches & Clothing-Optional Resorts

Is public nudity legal on the beaches?

> Public nudity is **not legal** on most beaches in Greece. However, there are some designated nudist beaches where nudity is allowed and accepted. These beaches are typically marked, and tourists should respect local customs and regulations. Outside of these areas, public nudity may lead to fines or legal issues. *For more details, see Chapter 19.*

Tourist Taxation

Is there room tax in Greece?

> **Yes.** Room tax (also known as the overnight stay tax) is imposed on visitors staying in hotels, apartments, and other accommodation types in Greece. The tax varies depending on the level of the accommodation and ranges from €0.50 to €4 (US$0.53 to $4.20) per night.

Is there any fee associated with leaving Greece?

> **No.** There is no exit tax for tourists when leaving the country. However, depending on your destination or airline, there may be other fees such as airport taxes or baggage fees, but these are not specific to leaving Greece itself. *For more details, see Chapter 22.*

Long-Term Stays

Do I need to return to my home country to apply for a work permit in Greece?

> **No.** As an American, you do not need to return to your home country to apply for a work permit in Greece. You can apply for a work permit while in Greece, but you must first secure a job offer from a Greek employer. Afterward, the employer typically handles the paperwork, and you may need to apply for a work visa at a Greek consulate if your application is approved.

As an American, how long can I stay in Greece without a visa?

As for how long you can stay in Greece without a visa, Americans can stay for **up to 90 days** within a 180-day period in Greece under the Schengen Area visa-free policy. If you wish to stay longer or work, you will need to apply for the appropriate visa or permit. *For more details, see Chapter 23.*

In the Event of Death

What documents would an embassy need regarding the death of a tourist?

In the event of a tourist's death in Greece, an embassy would typically need the deceased's passport, a medical certificate of death, the death certificate issued by Greek authorities, and identification documents from both the deceased and the informant. The embassy can assist with the documentation process, facilitate repatriation, and coordinate with local authorities. *For more details, see Chapter 25.*

EMERGENCY/IMPORTANT CONTACT NUMBERS IN GREECE

 Please consider putting some of these numbers in your phone prior to traveling to Greece.

Emergency Numbers:

- **Police:** 100
- **Fire:** 199
- **Ambulance:** 166

Other Useful Contacts:

- **General Emergency Services:** 112

  This is the universal European emergency number and can be dialed free of charge from any phone, including mobile phones.

- **Tourist Police (Athens):** 171
- **Coast Guard:** 108
- **Roadside Assistance:** 104 (Emergency breakdown assistance in Greece)

Legal Assistance:

- **Athens Bar Association:** +30 210 3398102-3
- **Legal Aid:** Available via local district courts or through legal assistance organizations in major cities.

USEFUL GREEK PHRASES

GREETINGS

HI/HELLO – Γειά σου (Yia sou)

GOOD MORNING – Καλημέρα (Kalimera)

GOOD AFTERNOON – Καλησπέρα (Kalispera)

GOOD NIGHT – Καληνύχτα (Kalinikhta)

GOODBYE – Αντίο (Adio)

MAGIC WORDS

PLEASE – Παρακαλώ (Parakalo)

THANK YOU – Ευχαριστώ (Efharisto)

YOU'RE WELCOME – Παρακαλώ (Parakalo)

CHEERS! – Στην υγειά σας! (Stin ygeia sas)

EXCUSE ME – Συγγνώμη (Signomi)

GETTING AROUND

WHERE IS THE BATHROOM? – Που είναι η τουαλέτα; (Pou einai i toualeta?)

WHAT TIME IS IT? – Τι ώρα είναι; (Ti ora einai?)

HOW DO I GET TO...? – Πως φτάνω στο...; (Pos ftano sto...?)

WHERE DOES THIS TRAIN/BUS GO? – Που πηγαίνει αυτό το τρένο/ λεωφορείο; (Pou pigei afto to treno/leoforeio?)

RESTAURANT – Εστιατόριο (Estiatorio)

HOW MUCH DOES THIS COST? – Πόσο κοστίζει; (Poso kostizei?)

TRAIN/METRO STATION – Σταθμός τρένου/μετρό (Stathmos trenou/metro)

COMMUNICATION

DO YOU SPEAK ENGLISH? – Μιλάτε Αγγλικά; (Milate Anglika?)

I DO NOT UNDERSTAND – Δεν καταλαβαίνω (Den katalavaino)

I DON'T SPEAK GREEK – Δεν μιλάω Ιταλικά (Den milao Italika)

I DON'T KNOW – Δεν ξέρω (Den xero)

EMERGENCY

HELP! – Βοήθεια! (Voithia!)

CALL AN AMBULANCE! – Καλέστε ασθενοφόρο! (Kaleste asthenoforo!)

I NEED A DOCTOR – Χρειάζομαι γιατρό (Chreiazomai giatro)

POLICE – Αστυνομία (Astynomia)

I'M LOST – Είμαι χαμένος/χαμένη (Ime hamenos/hameni)

IT'S AN EMERGENCY – Είναι έκτακτη ανάγκη (Ine ekstakti anangi)

GLOSSARY

ACQUITTAL: A jury verdict that a criminal defendant is not guilty, or the finding of a judge that the evidence cannot support a conviction.

ADVERSARY PROCEEDING: A lawsuit arising from a controversy that begins with filing a complaint.

AFFIDAVIT: A written statement made under oath.

APPEAL: A request made after a trial court has decided against one party in which the losing party asks a higher court to review the decision for legal error.

ARRAIGNMENT: A proceeding in which a criminal defendant is brought to court, told of the charges, and asked to plead guilty or not guilty.

BAIL: The temporary release of a person from jail when awaiting trial, on condition that a sum of money be lodged or deposited to guarantee an appearance in court.

BARRISTER: A lawyer admitted to plead at the Bar and who may try cases in superior court.

BURDEN OF PROOF: The duty to prove disputed facts.

CAUSE OF ACTION: A legal claim in a civil action.

COMPLAINT: A written statement that begins a civil lawsuit in which the plaintiff details the claims.

CONTRACT: An agreement between two or more persons to do something or to not do something.

CONVICTION: A judgment of guilt against a person charged with a crime.

CUSTOMS DUTY: A tariff or tax imposed on goods when transported across international borders.

COURT LIAISON: A person that coordinates with attorneys to perform administrative duties, such as scheduling witnesses, sharing information with law enforcement, and overseeing the reporting of cases to foreign embassies when applicable.

DAMAGES: Money that a defendant pays to a plaintiff in a civil case if the plaintiff wins.

DEFENDANT: 1) The individual against whom a civil claim is filed; 2) The individual against whom a criminal claim is filed.

FELONY: A serious crime, punishable by more than one year in prison.

MAGISTRATE: A judicial officer of a district court, who conducts initial proceedings in criminal cases, decides criminal misdemeanor cases, conducts many pretrial civil and criminal matters on behalf of district judges, and decides civil cases with the consent of the parties.

MISDEMEANOR: An offense punishable by one year or less in jail.

PLAINTIFF: A person or business that files a formal complaint with the court.

PLEA: In a criminal case, the answer of "guilty," "not guilty," or "no contest" in response to a criminal charge.

SOLICITOR: A lawyer who advises clients, represents them in lower court, and prepares cases for barristers to try in higher courts.

SOVEREIGN IMMUNITY: A legal doctrine by which the sovereign or the state (i.e. government) cannot commit a legal wrong and thus, it is immune from criminal and civil liability and cannot be sued.

STATUTE: A written law passed by a legislative body.

STATUTE OF LIMITATIONS: A statute prescribing a period of limitation to bring certain types of legal actions. If the action is not brought within that time, the person or entity (in a criminal context) is permanently barred from suing in court.

SUBPOENA: A command, issued under court authority, for a witness to appear and to give testimony.

TESTIMONY: Evidence presented orally by witnesses.

VERDICT: The decision of a judge or jury in a case.

WARRANT: Court authorization to conduct a search or to make an arrest.

ACKNOWLEDGMENTS

This book series would never have seen the light of day without the able assistance of the following people:

Kathy Adams, my paralegal for over 22 years, who is the "Best" I've ever worked with during my entire legal career because of her amazing work ethic, organizational skills, and her ability to think outside of the box in unique and creative ways;

Ally Knez-Siddique, a professional writer, and one of my paralegals, whose eye for detail, according to her, is both a blessing and a curse;

Gino Ibanez, my former law clerk, whose exceptional research skills helped move this book series along in its early stages;

Rosa Diaz Graham, my legal assistant who helped with research and word processing at the very beginning of this project;

Shelia Martin, one of my former paralegals, worked diligently on this series of books, even after taking on another job. Her organizational skills are reflected throughout;

Oliver Clark, whose hard work and diligence researching and writing, helped bring this book to life.

Mindy Scarlett, my marketing and publishing "Guru"! Her creativity and vision have no boundaries!

ABOUT THE AUTHOR

Michael L. Moore practices in Orlando, Florida, the city where he spent his formative years. He credits the trauma of having his brother murdered when he was only 10 years old, as the catalyst that drew him into the practice of law.

Moore attended Florida State University, where he was a member of the FSU debate team. Upon graduating, he was awarded a full scholarship to attend the University of Tennessee College of Law, where he was elected President of the Student Bar Association. He further honed his advocacy and public speaking skills by participating in 'moot court' competitions.

After clerking at the Tennessee Attorney General's office while in law school, Moore moved back to Orlando, Florida, to work at the State Attorney's Office as a prosecutor, and where he was fortunate enough to meet the young lady that would eventually become his wife. Moore moved on to working for private law firms, both local and national, and eventually established his own law firm in 1999. He continues to make Orlando his home base.

It was the murder of a close friend and client in Jamaica that caused Moore to realize that books on laws in other countries were few and far between, and he was inspired to create Law of the Land Publishing. Moore launched Law of the Land Publishing to provide a series of guidebooks and a membership site for tourists and business travelers to stay up to date on the laws in each country they travel to, as well as having access to assistance if they run into legal issues.

"My vision is to educate people on what their legal rights are, and how they can access legal assistance, no matter where they have to travel to in the world," said Moore. "As Americans, we have a right to due process, but in some countries, you don't even have the right to access a square meal when incarcerated. My goal is to provide the information needed to stay out of trouble, as well as having access to assistance if trouble finds you."

www.ingramcontent.com/pod-product-compliance
Lightning Source LLC
Chambersburg PA
CBHW051137120626
46547CB00012B/847